A MAN FROM LATVIA

ANDREJS EGLITIS

Golden Village

1995

INFINITY
PUBLISHING.COM

Copyright © 2009 by Andrejs Eglitis

ISBN 978-0-7414-5172-9

Published by:

PUBLISHING.COM

1094 New DeHaven Street, Suite 100
West Conshohocken, PA 19428-2713
Info@buybooksontheweb.com
www.buybooksontheweb.com
Toll-free (877) BUY BOOK
Local Phone (610) 941-9999
Fax (610) 941-9959

Printed in the United States of America

Printed on Recycled Paper

Published October 2012

DEDICATION

This book is dedicated to my children and grandchildren so you will know about a small country in Europe from where your roots come.

Andrejs

A Special thank you

To my Son & Daughter-in law
Imants and Cristina Eglitis
for their efforts to get this
book published.

Chase

Deanna

Justin

Brittanie

Brandon

Brent 1996

Duncan

MY GRANDCHILDREN

Give me your tired, your poor,
   Your huddled masses, yearning to breathe free,
The wretched refuse of your teeming shores,
   Send these, the homeless, tempest-tossed, to me;
I lift my lamp beside the golden door.

Emma Lazarus
Inscription on the Statue of Liberty

1

"Approaching Sterling, Sterling Illinois; prepare to depart the train at Sterling, next stop." The conductor walked briskly down the aisle, and stopped by the sleeping young man wearing a placard around his neck. The conductor had been instructed to be sure the young man departed the train at Sterling. He was quickly awake and felt a rush of anticipation at the thought of the new adventure he was beginning. He had been in the U.S. for less than two days. He was still not sure he was really here. He realized that this was another in the series of strange adventures that had begun for him more than seven years ago when he had left his parents' home. Finding himself in a situation he could never have dreamed of a few years ago was nothing new. Nevertheless, he was very excited about this new life he was starting. An ocean and many miles separated him from his home and family. There was no turning back now.

As the train pulled into the small, dark station, the young man, now wide awake, picked up the small bag containing his few possessions and stepped off the train. The conductor said "Good luck, young man," even though it was not clear he could be literally understood. The conductor had seen other such young people ride his train and had often wondered about them and what had brought them to this train ride. Some had seemed very timid and fearful, but not this one. He had an air of excitement and confidence that seemed to bode well for his future. Still, the conductor knew that luck and much more were needed for success in a new life, apparently alone, and with few language skills.

The two other people who left the train at Sterling soon disappeared into the dark night, and the young man found himself alone waiting for someone who he had hoped would be waiting for him.

After twenty or thirty minutes alone in front of the station he went inside and approached the sleepy-looking man at the window. Since he could not ask, "Where are my sponsors?" he pointed to the placard which told his name: Andrejs Eglitis, his home country: Latvia, USSR, and his sponsor's name: Sterling Steel & Wire Co., and their phone number. The man at the window obligingly called the number, and after a short conversation indicated that someone would arrive at about eight o'clock in the morning. Without much common language, the two were able to agree that the young man would sleep on a station bench until morning, which was yet several hours away. He was also very hungry, but had nothing left of the five dollars he had been given for food during the two-day train trip. He ignored the hunger pangs; he had been hungry for much longer periods. There was no place to buy food anyway. He was not apprehensive that no one was there to meet him. During the past few years he had become very pragmatic and had learned to deal with life's crises one by one. His youthful optimism assured him that everything would be all right as soon as he started his job at Sterling Steel & Wire Co., which had been promised him through the Immigration Office. He felt confident that the years of technical training at home and also while in the DP (Displaced Persons) Camp in Germany had prepared him for the work place. He had worked hard to be accepted at the Technical School at home and while he attended there. His parents had somehow instilled in him those important but elusive traits, self esteem and confidence. He had, in the seven years since he left home, proved to himself that he could deal with life on almost any terms and survive. He had reason to feel that luck was on his side. In spite of the uncertainty of the days ahead he was not afraid. Using his small bag for a pillow he fell immediately into a deep sleep.

At about eight o'clock he awoke to find two strangers standing over him. He followed them to their car, and they drove him to Sterling Steel & Wire Co. in Sterling. He couldn't talk much with them, but he tried to answer their questions as best he could. He could understand some English, but trying to speak was much more difficult. At the company, the men turned him over to a man in the employment office who showed him to his work place. The work was easy to understand and appeared easy enough to do. He had no fear that he could not do it.

He was still very hungry. He was given an advance of a week's salary so he could rent a room and buy some food. A driver was made available to help him. He needed a place close to work as he would walk to and from the workplace. Finding an appropriate room was simple enough, as was settling in. His few possessions fit in the corner of one dresser drawer, but he was not concerned about his lack of things. He was safe now and had the necessities of life: a home, a job and food. Always in the back of his mind was a nagging and sometimes raw sadness about his home country and the parents and small brother he had left behind. He knew that he dared not communicate with them, although he had a driving urge to do so; it was just too dangerous for them. After his last conversation with his parents, he had known that his life in Latvia was probably over, and that they wanted him to make the best possible life for himself. He was determined to do so. For the past seven years he had grown up rapidly; he knew that there is not much room for sentimentality in the pursuit of survival.

His daily routine was simple in his first months in the U.S. He had some difficulty in establishing a sleep schedule, as his work shift changed weekly, so he was sleepy all the time. However, the lack of fear and hunger made his work schedule seem a small inconvenience. He mostly just worked, ate and slept, and saved as much money as possible. He was an energetic worker and very thrifty, so that in three months he had repaid the cost of his train ticket and the five dollars he had been given. In another six months he saved enough to buy an old car. It was the first car he had ever owned and the first private car he had ever driven. He had obtained an international driver's license while still in Europe and had driven many vehicles, but having a car of his own was a dream realized. While he was growing up there had been few cars in evidence. He began to improve in the use of English and was soon communicating on a basic level.

One day, a few weeks into his new life, he was told by an acquaintance at work that there was a Latvian couple in Sterling who worked for the Lutheran Church, which was also their sponsor. The prospect of meeting people who spoke his language and shared his background was so appealing that he was soon knocking on their door. Marta and Karlis were overjoyed to meet someone from home. Karlis had been an architect in Latvia, but like many immigrants, was reduced to janitorial and maintenance work in the U.S. For Karlis, apparently the benefits of his new life were enough to compensate for the loss of his profession, as neither he nor his wife ever complained. They had made the choice to seek a new life and a better chance for their children, and they appeared satisfied with their choice. They introduced Andrejs to their church, and he was friendless no more. Soon two other young Latvian men began working at Sterling Steel & Wire Co., and they also became friends with Karlis and Marta. A small informal Latvian community had been established.

Since Andrejs was the only one of the group who owned a car, the others prevailed upon him to drive them all to Chicago for the November 18 Latvian Independence Day celebration, to which Marta and Karlis had been invited. Although Latvia had again been invaded by Communists, the Latvians still celebrated this significant day in their history, and got together in fellowship and unity.

The evening was wonderful, full of singing, conversation, and the food they all loved. Andrejs felt the warmth of Latvian hospitality and his ties to his country. The twenty or so people sang old familiar songs and reminisced about life in their country and in the DP Camp in Germany, where most of them had spent some time. Very late that night the young woman who was seated next to Andrejs stated that she had stayed too long and had missed the last bus. Andrejs did not know his way around Chicago, but in the spirit of rescuing a damsel in distress said, "I will be happy to drive you home if you will show me the way." She lived with an attorney's family as a household helper while also going to school. With her help and directions they finally got her home. She invited him to spend the night in the spare room. Her employers were surprised to find a handsome young man there the next morning. They invited him for breakfast, and after a pleasant meal with them, he found his way back to his friends. It seems that this could have been the beginning of Andrejs' first U.S. romance, but it was not. The young man was not led easily into a romantic involvement. He had the single-minded goal of establishing himself in his new country, and had no thought of romance. This focus on whatever goal he is pursuing has been characteristic of him throughout his life, and no doubt was instrumental in leading him through the many dangerous times he encountered.

He had kept up a correspondence with a Latvian friend, Rolands, whom he had known in the DP Camp. Rolands and his wife, Dzidra, and parents-in-law lived in Fon du Loc, Wisconsin, on a farm, and they worked in a cheese factory. One day Andrejs received a letter from Rolands asking, "Could you come in two weeks for the christening of our new son, and would you consent to be his godfather?" Having a car made many things possible, and Andrejs replied immediately, "I would be happy and honored; I'll be there." When he pulled out after work for the approximately two hundred mile trip to Wisconsin, snow was predicted. By eight o'clock the roads were snow covered and the experience was harrowing. He could only guess where the road was by the placement of electrical poles. In spite of the weather and the unpredictability of his car, Andrejs managed to arrive at his destination very late that night. His friends had long since decided that he would not be able to make it, and were astounded when he arrived. The baby, who was christened the next day, was named Andris and is now a chemist.

Rolands' wife, Dzidra, had a sister, Rasma, living in Milwaukee. Her husband, Bruno, worked in a foundry, and Rolands secured a job there through him. Rolands, however, had aspirations beyond the foundry, and after the day's hard work went to night classes at Marquette University, eventually graduating as a civil engineer.

Dzidra Kuplens had been a student in the DP Camp also. There had soon been an attraction and romance between Dzidra and Rolands. Everyone at school thought that they were a nice couple.

After graduating from the DP Camp school, Rolands had decided to join the U.S. Army and was in the same unit as Andrejs, stationed close to the city of Gussen. This was some distance from the DP Camp and from Rolands' sweetheart, but the distance didn't interfere with their relationship; about a year later they got married.

Dzidra's father, Zanis Kuplens had also joined the army, and Andrejs had the opportunity to know him better. Zanis had been a Latvian soldier who had fought Germans and Russians in 1918 during the chaos of the Russian Revolution and had helped to free their country from foreign rulers. Independence was proclaimed November 18, 1918. Andrejs admired this man, who was willing to die for a better future for the children. Without Zanis and other Latvian soldiers who had joined the newly formed Latvian Army so many years ago and fought for freedom, Andrejs knew he wouldn't have been able to enjoy his childhood and growing-up years in a free country.

There was a common understanding that a sponsored immigrant should stay for a year before moving from the place his sponsor had secured for him. It became clear to Andrejs that he would be moving on when his year in Sterling was completed; he also had ambitions.

For the first few months he lived in the room he had originally secured. Later he was offered a nicer place by an elderly couple he met at church, and he stayed there for a few months. Then Marta and Karlis were able to buy an old house and urged him to live with them. Moving was not difficult, as he still had few possessions.

Soon he heard of the move to Milwaukee by Rolands and his family, and of Rolands' pursuit of a college degree. This seemed to Andrejs a good plan, as he was also very much motivated to obtain more education and especially a degree in engineering. He still loved aviation, and would have become a commercial pilot if that were possible. However, after the war, the United States had a surplus of returning pilots, and he had no connections. He decided that he had a much greater chance of becoming an engineer. He made the decision to move to Milwaukee, and Rolands and Dzidra invited him to stay with them while he looked for a job and a place to live.

Karlis and Marta were very sad to see him leave Sterling. Their last evening together with the other Latvian friends was a bitter-sweet party. They all rejoiced at the success of their new lives, but mostly it was a sad farewell to Andrejs. Marta had tears in her eyes as she wished him, "Goodbye and good luck." It was much like a family member leaving the security of home to strike out on his own.

Andrejs' life so far had occasioned several sad goodbyes, and he had become somewhat stoic about them. No sad parting could ever match the pain of leaving his homeland and family. He moved on to another new beginning.

2

The year 1925 was a good time to be born in Latvia, and Andrejs was fortunate that he experienced his childhood while his country was independent and economically stable. More often than not, Latvia has been ruled by foreign powers.

The Latvians, along with the Lithuanians, have lived in the eastern Baltic region since ancient times. Their languages are somewhat similar. In the 13th century, Latvia was conquered and Christianized by the Germanic Knights of the Sword; their successors, the Teutonic Knights, founded the German-ruled state of Livonia, which dominated the region until the mid-16th century. In 1561-62 Latvia was divided between Poland and the Duchy of Courtland. The Swedes then occupied part of the country in the 17th century, and between 1720 and 1721 the whole region was conquered by Russia in the Great Northern War. Latvia was for many years a part of the German controlled medieval Livonia and later (1721-1918) of Tsarist Russia. A Latvian nationalist movement emerged in the 19th century, and independence was finally gained after the 1918 collapse of the Russian Empire.

When the Russian Revolution began in 1917, Latvia was under the thumb of the Russian Czar, as it had been for many years. Andrejs' father was inducted into the Russian military service. Twenty-five years later, his son was forced into the German military to fight against the Russians, who were then Communists.

Small countries like Latvia have had no ability to defend or fight for their own interests, but have been time and again pawns of larger countries. The invaders demanded these small countries' wealth and resources, their young men and their allegiance. It is difficult to imagine occupied countries having any allegiance to their invaders. However, fear can accomplish many things, and the threat of death and of reprisals against their families caused most young men to meet their invaders' demands, which in 1941 in Latvia meant fighting for the Germans. They never had the Latvians' allegiance, but only their surface acquiescence.

The last Latvian president, Karlis Ulmanis, was educated in the United States and received a Ph.D. from the University of Nebraska. He returned to Latvia in 1932 and became president. He apparently brought modern thinking and progressive ideas with him, and the Eglitis family was doing well until the Communists came in 1940.

During the period of freedom, from 1918 to 1940, Andrejs spent the first fifteen years of his life. Then the Second World War came to Latvia, in the form first of Communist Russia and then Nazi Germany. Andrejs remembers a time when there were armed German soldiers at one end of the street and armed Communists at the other, with his family in-between. They could not imagine then what would happen to their lives and their country because of a war they neither wanted nor understood. This situation has existed, of course, in many other times and places. It seems the human population of the world consistently produces a few people so greedy for power that many lives must be sacrificed in their quest.

So, the Russian Red Army invaded in 1940. Then in 1941 the German military force pushed the Russians out, and the country was German-occupied for several years until the end of World War II, at which time the Communists again took control.

Through all the centuries of occupation the Latvian people retained their identity, their language, and strong feelings of solidarity. When the USSR dissolved in 1992 they were emotionally ready and eager to be independent. They are now struggling to get the Russians out of their country after a long occupation.

Janis ("J" sound like "Y"), Andrejs' father, and Anna, his mother, seem to have had a happy marriage, and the household was a peaceful one. At least, Andrejs remembers it that way, without stress or tension. He remembers a happy childhood -- in good weather playing around the beach, in summer going to his relatives' farms, in winter playing all kinds of snow sports, building gliders and learning to play the violin. The latter did not much please him at the time, but nonetheless added music to his store of knowledge and a rich dimension to his life. As he went through his teens he qualified himself for Technical School, and developed an intense fascination for aviation, as he unknowingly prepared himself for a future he could not foresee.

Janis Eglitis worked for the Police Department for many years. His first love, though, was music, and he played the clarinet in the department orchestra. They performed in all kinds of local ceremonies and celebrations, such as parades and summer concerts in the park. He spent part of each day on Police Department business and also practiced with the orchestra. In addition, he practiced daily at home. Besides his clarinet, he played piano, mandolin, and violin. He was learning to play the bass as he hoped to join the city opera orchestra. Andrejs believes that his dad's dream for him was that he become a concert violinist. It was not to be.

Janis was a versatile person. In addition to music, he loved art and had talent as an artist; his painting of the "Last Supper" hung in their home. He raised beautiful flowers, as well as fruits and vegetables in his yard and in a greenhouse he had built. He had a woodworking shop where he built small things for the house and yard. He maintained his property, which consisted of a four-plex, one of the apartments of which was occupied by his family; the others were rented. He liked to play chess and cards with his friends, when they all practiced speaking Russian. They had all learned the language in the Russian army. Andrejs is amused when he remembers his father and friends speaking Russian. For quite a few years, he thought they were speaking in this foreign language so he couldn't understand what they were saying. When he got a little older, his dad assured him that the men were speaking Russian only for practice. When his dad and these other men were in the Russian army, they were very much alone and were forced to learn Russian. In contrast, Andrejs was in one way fortunate; in the German military his whole squadron was made up of Latvians, so he wasn't forced to speak German, and didn't feel so alone.

Anna was a devoted wife and mother, and Andrejs' memories of her are warm ones, but it is clear she was not the guiding light of his life. Most of what he remembers of his mother has to do with her duties as a homemaker and care-giver. The person whose guidance he followed and whose wisdom he most respected was his father. It is sad that his father was never to see the man that Andrejs became. In learning about Janis, a portrait of Andrejs emerges. He is also versatile and multi-talented. He admired his father very much and in many ways emulates his memory. A mother's influence on her children should not be minimized, however, and it is clear that Anna provided a warm and secure home for her son which fostered many of the traits of character that prepared him for the ordeals of his life.

Andrejs was raised as an only child until he was thirteen and a half, when his parents presented him with a baby brother, Vilnis. Since Andrejs was at home for only four more years, the brothers did not have time to know each other very well. Also, the difference in their ages precluded the possibility of their spending much time together.

Life in Latvia during Andrejs' childhood was much slower and simpler than the life we experience in the United States today. Of course, fifty years ago life here was likely less stressful and frantic than it seems now. For one thing, almost no women worked outside the home when Andrejs was a boy, and he never knew any couple to divorce. Everyone worked hard to make a living and a good home; the roles for each family member were quite clearly defined. Life seems to be less stressful when each person knows what is expected of him or her, and options are limited. Of course, this more old-fashioned way of life does not allow for the maximum development of each person's talents and abilities, and women in particular had almost no chance to become other than wives and mothers. However, it is probably simpler and more orderly for the society as a whole. There is no way to know if people in general or as individuals were more or less happy and satisfied with their lives than people today in the United States -- and many other countries -- where so many choices are available. This question often comes to mind as we hear of Andrejs' happy childhood with a mother always at home to provide whatever was needed for her family. Is that still the best way? and for whom? It's a complicated question.

When hearing about all the immigrants Andrejs knew on his way here, and since he arrived, the number of success stories is quite remarkable. So many of them came here with nothing except perhaps a very sad heart for those who had to be left behind. Many of them have been unusually successful in business or have achieved a high degree of education and the good life that usually implies.

They have been highly motivated and hard-working. One wonders whether those of us born here have the same degree of ambition and courage (or whatever it takes) to survive and prosper in spite of very hard times. Did these immigrants have some special in-born strength or did they just rise to the occasion? Could we do as well if faced with the fear and loss they endured? There is no answer, or at least we have no way of knowing it. We hope we will never have to confront our country's being torn apart by war or its invasion by an enemy. It is certainly true that our country has been made stronger by the strength and courage of so many who, like Andrejs, have come here seeking a new life. Perhaps because of their hardships to get here, they have brought an unusual degree of ambition and hope.

All the many thousands who have found their way here and embraced this country as their new home -- including all our ancestors -- probably would have much to tell us if they only could. Most of the people are gone, as are their stories.

Recorded here are the memories of a certain Latvian man whose life was drastically and unexpectedly changed by events of history over which he had no control. This is the story of a survivor.

3

Andrejs speaks: Once I was a little boy playing soccer barefoot and pulling girls' hair in school, and in the spring taking rides on pieces of broken ice along the Baltic Sea shore. During winter my parents had a hard time to keep me inside the house. I liked to ice skate, ski, play ice hockey on the pond, and build snowmen with charcoal eyes and carrot noses. Of course, we had snowball fights. My parents bought me ice skates and skis, but most of our playing equipment we made.

I always tried to postpone my homework until darkness ended our daytime play.

Early summer sunburns that I got by playing by the sea were my suffering for many years. My parents always told me to be more careful and to remember how I felt last year, but I guess when I started playing I forgot all about being careful, and every year I had a new sunburn. I was very lucky that I had a mother who was home any time I needed her, and she always had lots of sour cream for my burns.

We lived in a nice house near the Baltic Sea. My parents owned a four family house, and we lived in one of the upstairs apartments and rented out the other three. We didn't have any indoor plumbing except for running water in the kitchen. There was an outhouse for each of the apartments. This was no problem in the daytime, especially in the summer. In the winter, though, we hoped we wouldn't have to go outside as it was miserably cold, sometimes below zero. It wasn't just that it was so cold, but snow fell almost continuously, so we would literally have to shovel our way to the outhouse, even in the middle of the night. I can't think of how we managed without a bathroom, but we didn't know anything different then, and we just lived with conditions as they were.

We had a kitchen and living room with a fireplace for heating. The houses there were built for cold weather and the fireplace had embers all night that kept the chill out. There were two small bedrooms. Until my little brother, Vilnis, was born I had one of the bedrooms to myself, but when he was old enough to leave my parents' room, he moved in with me. I didn't mind; I was used to another boy in the family by that time. I looked forward to his growing up a little so he could go out with me. I had no idea that our time as room-mates would be so short.

In retrospect, I guess it was really just a small apartment and quite ordinary, but I thought it was a fine home, and I was happy there.

I think I was lucky, as I have often heard of people who grew up surrounded by their parents' animosity and stress, often about money, but this was not my life. I never heard my parents argue or even just talk about money. We seemed to get along fine, and I never thought of the family's finances or any other problems they might have.

We ate in the kitchen where my mom cooked on a wood stove. We didn't have an ice box, but the weather is cold in Latvia a good part of the year, and she managed with the help of our deep cellar.

We raised a large part of our own food. My dad had a garden with flowers and vegetables, and we had fruit trees. We had a goat which furnished most of our milk for drinking. One of my jobs was to take the goat out in the morning and tether her near some grass. In the afternoon I would milk her before dinner. I had many small responsibilities around the house.

We ate fish a lot of the time. Being so near the Baltic Sea, we caught some of what we ate, but fish was also available from the commercial fishermen coming in. We also ate salted herring bought at the store and smoked herring from the smokery. Sometimes my dad and I went fishing, and I loved those times.

One of my jobs was to go to the store to do the small shopping for things we could not raise, such as beef, butter, flour and sometimes bread or cows' milk. The store was not just a place to buy food. It was also the meeting place of the neighborhood, and all the little news and gossip were exchanged there. I was always happy when my mom sent me there, as I liked to see all the people, and I was often given a treat by the lady who ran the store.

We had nothing like Coke or 7-Up, but we loved what we had -- birch tree juice on ice. The farmers extracted the juice by cutting a plug an inch around in the trunk. A hole was drilled through the plug; then it was returned to the tree. A bucket was left by the tree to catch the juice when it dripped from the hole in the plug. The juice was stored in the cellar for special occasions. The hole in the tree was permanently plugged, and the tree suffered no effect.

Another drink that was a favorite was made from milk. First, whole milk was left to sour. During the souring process it separated into liquid on top and solid on the bottom. The solid was yogurt and was also used to make cottage cheese. The liquid was like water with a light greenish color and was mixed with a little non-fat milk and barley to thicken it. In a few days it was ready to drink. We loved the slightly sour taste; we called this drink "putra." We didn't have any of the soft drinks that American children are used to. We drank milk with meals and water or putra the rest of the time. Putra was stored in a large container in the kitchen and was available almost all the time.

My mom canned everything possible and made jelly, pickles, sauerkraut and anything else she could find to get us through the winter. We stored potatoes, carrots and onions in the cellar.

Since there was no refrigeration, the store used blocks of ice from the sea for the things that had to be kept cold. We salted and dried meat and fish as soon as possible to preserve them.

Each morning my mom was the first one up and she started the fire in the kitchen for cooking and a good fire in the fireplace for heating the house. She made my breakfast and got me off to school. I usually had left-over fried potatoes, salted or smoked herring, goats' milk, and bread and jelly. She also insisted that every morning I have a raw egg. I poked it in the end with a needle, and sucked the contents out. I also had to have a spoonful of fish oil before I went to school. I remember this ritual fondly, although the fish oil was hard to take. I quit the egg and fish oil the day I left home.

In the fireplace there was a hot plate surface built in for keeping food hot and warming up soup, tea, and milk. I liked to drink hot milk with honey in it. Real coffee was very expensive to buy; it had to be imported. My family did not drink it. Some people ground roasted chestnuts as a substitute for coffee. Natural tea made from dried out blooms of various trees was the most popular drink after people had been outside in the cold weather.

A snack that we loved was very similar to what we call potato chips. Very thin slices of potato were placed on the hot plate until they became brown and crispy.

My dad raised special cucumbers to be made into pickles, and my mom made very good ones. The cucumbers were placed in a barrel in the cellar for pickling between layers of leaves and spices, especially dill. The whole barrel was filled with water and vinegar over the cucumbers. A circular wood disk with a heavy rock was placed on top and left while they processed into pickles. I've forgotten all the details, but I remember the pickles; I'm still looking for a pickle as good as my mom used to make. They were used all year long from the barrel. I will admit that sometimes they disappeared pretty fast, as I loved them and sneaked quite a few out of the barrel while my parents were still waiting for the pickling process to be completed. We had a farmers' market nearby. My dad didn't raise cabbage, so we bought it in the market. All of us worked to make it into sauerkraut because it was a big job to shred enough cabbage to fill the wood barrel used to process it in.

In the fall Dad purchased a whole pig from the farmer and had it processed by cutting it into pieces for smoking. Pork sausages were made using pig intestines as the casing and filling these with ground meat, spices and some other ingredients. Sausages were smoked at the same time as the rest of the meat. Blood sausage was very well-liked and was made by mixing ground pork meat with barley and blood. Blood sausage was slightly smoked and fried before serving and was very popular for breakfast. Pigs' heads were smoked and saved for the New Year's Eve celebration. Pig legs, boiled in water, produced their own gelatin; before it started gelling the meat was cut off the bone and placed into the liquid to harden. This meal was served with mustard, vinegar and rye bread with butter. All bones were saved for making soups, such as potato, red beet, sauerkraut and vegetable.

It was a good feeling that our cellar was filled with food we had prepared at home and that nothing had been wasted. Only a few items we had to buy from the store.

For special occasions, my mom made rice-raisin soup. I thought it was a real treat, and I guess it was, because the ingredients had to be imported and were therefore expensive.

Another very special treat, also imported, was oranges. Sometimes when I wasn't feeling well or for a special occasion, my dad would come home with an orange for me. Never did I imagine that in my life I would be able to have rice, raisins and oranges every day if I wanted.

One thing we did have in abundance, which I still like, was sunflower seeds. My dad grew large sunflowers about six feet tall, and when the seeds in the center got dark, we'd cut the heads and remove the seeds. They were dried in the sun and mom roasted them. They were a popular snack then, and they are still one of my favorite between-meal foods.

My mom was a medicine woman. She knew roots, leaves, and flowers that were needed for different illnesses. Usually different roots in combination with other ingredients were put in several containers and filled with alcohol; these were placed on a window sill and, with the sun's help, medicine was created. We rarely saw a doctor; my mom could cure just about anything.

My mom did the laundry, with just a little help from me. The laundry facilities were in a separate building. A large round cast iron tub about four feet in diameter and two feet deep was built into a concrete fireplace, and two rectangular smaller tubs with hand operated rubber wringers were attached to it. The tubs were bolted to the concrete floor, where there was a water drain hole. A table was placed close to the tubs for handling the laundry. Several clotheslines were stretched between the walls, and more were available outside.

We had four families living in our building, and a laundry day was assigned to each family, and the additional two days were available for whoever needed them. No one did laundry on Sundays.

Outside the building was a large hand water pump about six feet tall with a four foot long wooden handle. It took about three to four strokes to fill up the bucket. The large tub was filled with water and slices of soap. Wooden logs were used for heating the tub. When the water was warm, laundry was placed into the tub and soaked for several hours. Actual washing was done by hand on a scrub board and then placed into the rinse water tub. The rinse tub water was replaced several times by bringing the buckets in with clean water from outside. After rinsing, the laundry pieces were pulled through the rubber rollers for squeezing the water out.

In good weather, the laundry was hung outside to dry. Most of the fabrics were wool, cotton and linen, which needed hand ironing. For this purpose an iron made of cast iron was used. The top opened and had a lid. The lid was opened and embers from the fireplace were put into the iron. In a few minutes, when the iron was hot enough, it was used to iron the clothes. Of course, the embers had to be replaced several times to keep the iron hot enough.

One of our neighbors had a unique large table press. For a small fee, we were allowed to use this for our larger pieces. The press was twice as long as a bed sheet. The roller table on top of the sheets was a box-like structure with rollers attached; the box was loaded with heavy rocks. The length of this table was about the length of the sheets. A large handle with a gear and pinion was attached to the heavy frame, so that the roller table could be moved back and forth. One of my jobs was to crank this machine. The laundry took a full day each week.

Our house was built of wood, and I'm not sure about the roof. I do know that every year my dad was on the roof for one long day re-coating it with hot tar. It was a two-story house with a double pitched roof and getting up there was very frightening and dangerous. For that reason my dad tied himself to the chimney while he did this job. He didn't let me on the roof, but I tended the tar on the ground. It had to be kept hot enough to maintain a thick liquid consistency. My dad made a pulley for hoisting the tar bucket up from the ground where I was keeping it the right temperature. When he was ready for some more up there, I filled the bucket with a heavy ladle and sent it up to my dad via the pulley.

Another job I did with my dad was preparing firewood for winter. He bought birchwood logs, and they had to be cut into the right sizes for the stove and fireplace. He used a two-man saw, and I was proud to be considered one of the men.

There was a concrete sidewalk in front of our house by the street. We had a white picket fence with a gate into our yard, and the concrete sidewalks continued to the left and right leading to doors to the four apartments. My dad had a beautiful flower garden on the left leading to his workshop and storage, which we called "the garden house." On the right side were clothes lines with the laundry room and the outhouses. The back yard was quite large, with cherry, apple, and pear trees, as well as the greenhouse my dad built where he raised vegetables. He also grew vegetables in the back yard. Across the street was our potato field.

Three houses down the street the road ended, and there was a path leading to a large unoccupied field. This was our neighborhood playground with grass growing wild. The most popular game was soccer, and grass didn't get much chance to grow where we played. We usually played soccer barefoot. Our school shoes would get quickly ruined playing; all the kids couldn't afford special soccer shoes with cleats, especially since our feet were growing rapidly. Usually, if one of us didn't have soccer shoes, we all played barefoot. We spent a lot of time barefoot anyway.

Later, when we grew older and got better at the game, some of us were chosen to play in the neighborhood school or city teams for various age levels. Then the teams provided soccer shoes and uniforms. I was proud to slip real soccer shoes on my feet.

The Baltic Sea was a great mystery to me as a child. My home was just back from the beach, and I spent a lot of time watching the big ships coming into the breakwater to wait their turn to come into the harbor.

The boys from my neighborhood liked to stand by as the ships were unloaded in the harbor if we didn't get chased away. We picked up anything that dropped. Our favorite cargo was coconuts. We all loved them and tried to beat our friends to the choice pieces. We also watched the ships being loaded with exports from our country. Live pigs, pulp-wood, birch plywood, butter and especially linen were packed onto the ships going to England, Germany, or places we didn't know about.

The sailors on the ships didn't speak our language, but sometimes they played with us and taught us to play baseball. We didn't have anything like a bat, but we used a flat board and a tennis ball.

Looking for amber was another thing I liked, and I spent many mornings doing this. Amber was our national stone and was formed many million years ago from the sap of pine trees that landed under the water. It got washed up from the Baltic Sea on the beach and was sometimes found in seaweed. It is used to make beautiful jewelry. There are only a few places in the world where amber can be found. I learned to make amber jewelry in 4-H club.

My friends and I had a favorite swimming place just inside the breakwater. We also fished there for eels, which were a delicacy. We took them home and our moms fried or smoked them.

One memory I have of that place is about a middle-aged red-headed man who often came there to swim. He would put his newspaper out on a rock in the breakwater. After his swim he would pick it up and float on his back for a long time reading his paper and not getting wet. He was the father of six children, and the first person I knew who disappeared from our neighborhood one night after the Communists came.

I can still so clearly remember the sights and sounds of the sea. Even though sixty years have passed, I haven't forgotten any of it; it was such a big part of my childhood. Fishing boats going to sea and returning with their catch, I remember well. From our dock most of the boats were rowed by three or four men. The fishermen had faces that were strong and weathered. Many of the paintings by artists at that time were of the boats or men. They left a strong memory with me. The sound of the waves rolling in and of the ships' horns, as well as the sight of the lighthouse guiding the ships are in my heart forever.

When I was about six years old my dad decided it was time to begin my musical education. My dad was a musician, although he worked at the Police Department also. A clear memory of my childhood is my dad practicing his clarinet. He decided I should play the violin; he bought me a three-quarter size one and began to teach me to play it. His main instrument was the clarinet, but he also played some other instruments, including the violin. He taught me for four years. My heart was not in it, and sometimes I was in tears because I didn't want to practice; I'd rather have been outside playing soccer or some other game with my friends. After my dad, I had a professional teacher for two more years. Part of the reason I disliked it was that I was allowed to practice only scales and techniques; I wanted to play songs. However, I kept up my rigorous practice schedule because I didn't want to make my dad unhappy. I always wanted to please him. I am sure he had high hopes for me as a musician, but his hopes could not become a reality. Even if I hadn't had to leave home, I don't believe I would ever have become a professional musician.

One of the events the kids all looked forward to was a parade. On one particular parade day, I was to march in my Cub Scout uniform. I had had a very bad cold for several days and my parents wanted me to stay home. They were sure I'd get sicker by going out. I wanted so much to march in my uniform I finally wore them down, but only because I promised to come right home. On my way home I saw some large, decorated, motorized fishing boats advertising free rides. I forgot my Boy Scout promise. I knew my parents would be angry and worried, but the ship called to me, and I couldn't resist; I went for a ride. I was prepared for punishment, but unbelievably a miracle happened. I got much better, and my cold was almost gone by the time I got home. My parents were so happy that I was better, and they never knew my secret. I escaped the punishment I expected.

Another time I did get in big trouble for not coming home when I should. The activities in the breakwater and harbor fascinated me so much, I would forget all about the time and stay by the water too long, so that my parents would be worried. They told me time after time to come home earlier, but I kept being late, so my dad finally decided I needed some help to remember; he took his belt to my backside. This was an unusual thing for him to do. I couldn't sit for a couple of days, but I remembered to come on time after that.

School was three or four miles from home, and there was no school bus. We walked. It took a lot of bundling up to face the daily walk in very cold weather. My mom taught me to protect my feet by wrapping them in newspaper; then I put on heavy socks and shoes. "Getras" went over the tops of the shoes with the pants tucked in for warmth. Rubber galoshes went on the outside to keep my feet dry.

Sometimes we could take a streetcar, but in the heavy snow, which lasted for most of the school year, the streetcar could not run. All of us neighborhood kids had some kind of skis and sometimes we skied to school. Once in a while we were able to hook onto the back of a horse-drawn sled or wagon for part of the way, being drawn over the snow on our skis.

Most of the time, my mom packed me a lunch of bread and meat or fish and cheese, but whenever I could talk her into giving me money, I bought a bagel, some cream cheese and a piece of halva. I loved halva so much; I though of it as sesame candy and it melted in my mouth. These foods I bought fresh at a Jewish bakery on the way to school.

I didn't like school much, mostly because it took me away from all that I thought was going on in my neighborhood. I also didn't like the walk in the cold.

We had to wear uniforms to school. These consisted of black wool pants and a jacket with a collar. There was also a white collar liner which had to be clean every day. Our outfit looked kind of like a priest's. In grade school there were both boys and girls. The girls wore black pleated skirts with straps and white blouses.

The teachers had a lot of authority. Discipline was much tougher than I observe in schools here today. The teachers had the final word. Sometimes they would have a collar inspection to see if our liners were clean. Occasionally they even went so far as to have us remove our shoes and socks to see if our feet and socks were clean. Our parents respected the schools and teachers, and would never protest the schools' authority over us.

My favorite subject at school was art. Since my brother, Vilnis, became an artist, I guess there were some artistic genes in our family. I also loved all sports.

I was in the 4-H Club and they had many good activities. We learned to plant a garden and to do basic wood-working. Of course, I learned a lot about these things from my dad also.

Once I remember that we were the winners in volleyball at a sports jamboree. We then got to go to a sports camp to compete. Going away from home was an unusual experience. I was about ten, I believe.

The Boy Scouts offered many things I liked too. I started as a Cub Scout and advanced to Boy Scout. One year there was an international jamboree with boys from many countries in Europe. It was held in our capital city, Riga, which has a beautiful white sandy beach. Most of the activities took place there. Each night we had a large campfire on the beach and we sang songs in our own language. Each country's scouts put on a performance for the rest. Our uniforms were very similar to those from all the different countries. Being a Boy Scout was one of the best things I remember from those years.

The camp was decorated with flags of all the countries participating in the jamboree. All the boys from different countries, for friendship and memories, traded Boy Scout pins and other small insignia.

The first English word I ever learned was "exchange," because of all the exchanging of Scout items we did there. English was kind of the common language, because the most recognized leader and many of the boys were from England. I never dreamed that English would become my main language some day.

We had a wonderful county fair in my city each summer. It was similar to the county and state fairs in the U.S. today. There were games and rides, including a merry-go-round.　　The traveling European circus performances were a big part of it. There was an organ grinder with his monkey on his shoulder holding a hat; when you put money in his hat the monkey jumped on top of the box. From a drawer the monkey picked out a message of wisdom for you. Secretly you had to read the message and believe what it said. It was kind of like the messages in fortune cookies we get at Chinese restaurants today.

There were many booths selling special foods. One of my favorite treats was a hexagonal tube of freshly made ice cream cone-like material filled with whipped cream. They also sold many candies, sausages, ice cream and other good things. We looked forward to the fair all year.

One interesting experience that I remember at the fair one year was seeing the first black person of my life. He was with the circus and was leading an elephant around the grounds as an attraction. I don't believe any black people lived in Latvia. Perhaps the weather was too cold for them after living in a hot country like Africa. After I saw him, I thought a lot about the differences in people, and wondered about Africa, where black people came from.

I don't remember having ice cream available at the farm or in small towns, but in the city on certain street corners or parks, the ice cream man was glad to sell scoops of it. We didn't have cones, but the scoops were placed between two round waffle disks which were held with two fingers, and the ice cream was licked between. I remember a number of times when I was on the farm that, after church on Sunday, the farmer said, "Let's take the kids to the city to have ice cream." I've heard that in some families in the U.S. going for ice cream was a family outing also.

From an early age -- maybe ten -- when I was in elementary school, some kids folded up pieces of paper and called them airplanes. They threw them in the air, and paper airplanes were flying all over. Sometimes they even landed where the boys wanted. The goal was to land them in a girl's hair.

At that time, air for me was only for breathing and nothing else. Everything that I dropped was falling straight down to the ground. Why a piece of paper folded a certain way was able to fly puzzled me. Folding paper airplane wing tips in different ways made it possible for an airplane to go up or down, left or right. My curiosity grew and I started to observe the bigger boys who were flying hand-held glider models made of wood. It was amazing to me how these gliders were built and how well they flew. I held them very carefully in my hands, and they were built so light that I could hardly feel their weight, but they were structurally very strong. A string was attached to the fuselage and when all conditions were right, the helper boy started running and the model glider started to climb. The faster the helper boy was running, the higher the glider went. It was the model glider free flight with no engine and propeller attached to it. It was beautiful to see the hand-made bird flying very gracefully and landing some distance away.

I had flown kites before with the strings attached to them, and with the wind's help they could fly pretty high in the air. We liked to send messages to the flying kites. The messages were pieces of paper with a hole in the middle and something written on them. The kite string was passed through the hole and the message started moving faster and faster on the string until it reached the kite. Sometimes we sent many messages. When the boy let the kite string loose the kite fell down to the ground. It didn't fly like the glider model when it reached the desired height after the boy released the string. A glider was designed for free flight; a kite wasn't.

At that time if we wanted kite or glider models we had to build them ourselves. They were not available in the stores. I wanted to build a glider model and I had to start from scratch and to learn the hard way. Some literature and plans on how to build model gliders were available in the stores, but I found out that the older boys' expert advice was the most helpful for selecting the right materials and techniques for building a glider. I wanted one, and I built it. As a big surprise to me, it flew. My reward was seeing it flying well. After the first one, the others were much easier to build, but they started getting more complicated, with impact detachable wings, multi-colored appearance and wing span of up to six feet.

Building these hand-made glider models was very tedious and demanding work, but it was great fun, and I learned a basic engineering principle -- how to use minimum material to create maximum strength.

Boys who were interested in building and flying these hand-held gliders were naturally attracted to one another, and we began trying to out-do each other. The competition stretched our creative abilities and added to the fun.

We also had some set-backs during our glider trials. Sometimes, after weeks of work, we'd go out prepared for a triumphant day; then the wind was too strong or something else, and the glider would crash. We'd have to start all over again.

I passed away many, many hours with my new friends building and flying glider models. I can see now how directly that interest led to the path my life took in a few years.

4

My father and mother each had eight brothers and sisters. Most of them lived on farms. When I was ten or eleven my parents decided I should spend my summer on one of the farms to get to know my relatives and to learn a little about farm life.

I was surprised to see children six or seven years old being given the total responsibility for certain farm chores, such as preparing food for and feeding the cows, horses and pigs. The children did not have to be told each time to do their jobs; they knew what they were and they did them.

My little cousins made whistles from twigs, wove baskets and took the cows out by themselves. I could see that it took everybody on the farm doing his job to make it all work.

I liked being on the farm even though I had to work much harder than I did at home. Even at my young age I admired the farmers and their families. They provided almost everything they needed for themselves.

They worked from sun up to sun down six days a week, but did only the minimum on Sunday, which was the day for church and rest. Most of the Latvian people were Lutheran.

During the winter, both men and women had plenty of work, even though there were no crops to harvest. The men processed the cow hides into leather during the summer, and in winter they used the leather to make shoes, harnesses, and other items around the farm. They felled trees and cut them into the lengths needed for stove and fireplace wood, as well as logs to be sent to the mill for cutting into lumber used for building improvements and other projects. The women knitted gloves, socks, and scarves, and made most of the other clothes for the family.

Very good linen was grown in our country, and seeing it growing and blossoming is a sight to remember. The flowers were deep lavender blue, and the fields where they were growing a couple of feet high were just beautiful. When the wind rippled through the linen field, it looked like gentle waves in the Baltic Sea. I could lie and watch it all day, it seemed so peaceful. However, on the farm there was no time to lie and watch anything for long.

Farmers harvested the linen by hand and made it into bundles, which were taken to the pond for a wet/sun dry process that bleached the fibers. Then they were sent to a textile factory to be made into cloth. When the linen came back to the farm, the farmer's wife took over and made the linen into shirts and other clothes.

The women did all the work in the house, and that included many tasks. There were none of the household conveniences that are now considered necessities. They made everything from soap to sausage, bread and clothing. Generally, all of this was done without electricity. Kerosene lamps were used for light, and wood was used for heating, cooking, and many other jobs. They used sewing machines, but these were manually operated.

There were huge ovens above a special fireplace in the kitchen where bread and baked goods were made once a week. I was fascinated to watch the women handle the huge, heavy bread dough, kneading and folding it over and over. They made several kinds of bread at once and also pastries with various fruit fillings. I had seen my mom make bread and pastries at home, but never like on the farm. The amount and variety needed for a week by a large family and additional farm workers was enormous. A huge, round loaf of bread, about sixteen inches across was consumed each day, and the oven was large enough to bake six to eight loaves at once. The women had a large, flat wooden tool for putting the bread into and out of the oven. At the same time the bread was baking the heat and smoke were used for other food preparation, such as smoking ham, sausage and bacon. The huge loaves of bread were so heavy I could hardly lift one. They were not full of air like some modern, commercial breads.

After the cows were milked, the milk for the household was kept cool by lowering it into the well in a closed metal container. When milk was needed for drinking or for making butter, yogurt, cheese, sour cream, etc., the container was pulled up. Caring for the milk and making the milk products was another large task of the females of the family. Feeding the hard-working family and farm workers was a major job. Some seasonal workers were hired, and these had to be fed and cared for also. It seems incredible now that as much work as food preparation was, it was only one part of the women's work. Everyone on the farm worked as hard as they were able.

Whenever the women did have time, especially during harvest, they helped out in the fields. Some of the workers who were hired for the harvest were women. One day there was an air of excitement among the workers; a baby was being born in the potato field. There was nothing like "maternity leave" for the women, and they kept working for as long as possible. I think maybe the hard work could make a baby come a little sooner than expected. If there was a midwife in the vicinity -- meaning a few miles away -- and if there was time, she was summoned. However, that was not so easy, as the horse and buggy had to be made ready for the trip, and the trip was slow. A birth was often assisted only by the women present. The men, even the father, were not involved in the birth until a squalling baby was ready to be presented.

I remember so much about the farm, I guess because it was so different from my normal life. At home, of course, I slept in my bed; on the farm my favorite sleeping place was the hay loft. I loved the clean, soft hay and the sounds of the animals below. Climbing up the ladder to the loft I felt like I was entering my own little world, with just the hay, the animals, and me.

Another thing I won't forget about the farm is the thunder storms. They were overwhelmingly loud and frightening, and the lightning that accompanied them was terrifying. They were preceded by a darkening sky looking very angry and forbidding. Soon the lightning and the rumbling thunder began, getting louder and louder. Whether I was in the loft or out on the farm, I looked for a ditch and jumped in to wait out the storm. To find a place below ground level and away from the storm was everyone's goal.

When I was at home, for some reason I don't remember the thunder and lightning as being so frightening. I do remember the sound of many ships' horns when a storm began. There was no such thing as radar, sonar or short wave radios to keep them from crashing into each other. Communication on the water was mostly by blowing ships' horns to announce their location, and by a Morse Code transmitter, which was a spotlight with a movable lid, so light could be released in prescribed intervals to send a message. When Morse Code was first devised it was considered a great step forward in communication at sea, but it was a long way from the sophisticated systems in use today.

In June of 1940 I was a city boy enjoying a few summer months on the farm. As always, I loved the farm and was looking forward to a good summer with the great feeling of peace and freedom I always had there. The fields, the animals, the farm family and wide blue sky contributed to the happy environment. I liked the feeling that I was part of it all. It was probably a good time for my mom to be relieved of my care for a while, as home had changed a lot in the past couple of years. My mom had given birth a year ago last November, and we now had a little boy to be cared for. My small brother's name was Vilnis.

One afternoon in early July I had a letter from my mom saying that I had been accepted at Technical School beginning that fall. I was happy, because I had been hoping very much to be accepted. Many more boys applied to that school each year than could attend, and I had kept my grades high and passed qualifying tests. I felt that what I learned there would be helpful in my later life, especially since I was very much interested in aviation and engineering.

Each school in Latvia had its own colors, which were worn on the cap. I would be very proud to wear the dark and light green of my new school. The school had only boys, so the distractions would be few. I was eager to begin. I should explain that this school was a five-year school for the grades that are equivalent to high school and early college in the United States.

Technical School offered three major fields of study: mechanical, electrical and architectural. Graduation in one of these fields gave a student admission to the University, which was extremely competitive. Graduation also assured an immediate job in industry. My field of study was mechanical.

Many students continued in regular high school, which we called gymnasium. Some would then go to university, and some would leave school and go into one of the trades or other jobs.

After I had been on the farm for two or three weeks that summer we all came in one day for our noontime meal and rest. On the farms everyone started work early. We had a light breakfast, often bread, cheese, and milk, which we carried to the fields with us. At about 11 a.m. we all headed for the house and our main meal of the day. While the weather was the hottest we rested for a couple of hours before returning to the farm work. We usually listened to the radio for the news at that time. On this day we started eating dinner and someone turned on the radio and said in a loud voice, "Quiet everyone. The president is on the radio; we need to hear this." Soon everyone was quiet and we heard our president speaking unbelievable words.

"Fellow Latvians, I have something to say that will affect all of us. I ask you please not to panic, but to prepare yourselves for a great change that is coming to our country. There is at present a heavy concentration of Russian Communist tanks at our border. I believe we must prepare for an immediate invasion. Estonia, Lithuania and Finland are in the same situation. Please stay tuned to your radios and I will make further announcements as I have information for you."

For the first few seconds after this announcement, those at our table sat in stunned silence. No one had dreamed of such a thing happening. The young people, such as I, had no knowledge of even the word "Communist." Our lives were carefree and we did not know what it meant to be invaded, except that it wasn't good. Most of the older people, though, knew that this was very bad news, and they soon began talking all at once, speculating on what was really happening and how it would or could affect our lives. They said to each other, "Maybe it isn't as serious as we fear, and we're worrying too much. We'll wait and see what he says later."

Of course, where there are animals and crops to care for, the humans cannot stay in the house all day. We reluctantly went back to our jobs. However, everyone hovered around the house as much as possible that afternoon, hoping to hear anything more from our president. Soon he did have chilling words for us. "An agreement has been made with Estonia and Lithuania that there will be no military resistance against the Communist invaders. The invasion has begun, and we cannot stop it. Please prepare yourselves as best you can. God be with our country and all of us in the days ahead."

After his message, the Latvian National anthem, "God Bless Latvia," was played for the last time.

Soon thereafter our president, Karlis Ulmanis, was taken by the KGB and sent to Siberia, where he died. It was the same fate experienced by many other Latvians who were later taken. More than 150,000 Latvians suffered deportation or death in the one year the Soviets occupied my country.

Everyone was stunned. Before this noon no one had any slight idea that we were on the verge of invasion by Russia. There was no warning. It was like thunder from a blue sky. I went to the farm for a couple of pleasant months that summer. Before I went home the radio delivered news that drastically changed my life forever.

There were no telephones at the farm or at home so I could not talk to my parents about all this. I needed my dad's reassurance that our lives would continue on as before. I felt very alone and frightened.

Everyone did the minimum work that afternoon after we heard our president's words. The rest of the day and evening were spent in talking and evaluating what we had heard. The adults understood that we had totally inadequate military resources to fight the invasion. Their feelings were of helplessness. They asked each other questions that no one could answer. What was going to happen to us and to our free country? How much did we need to fear the invaders? Why did the Russians want our small country?

The Fins had decided that they would defend their border and were prepared to fight the Russians. Finland is geographically in a much better position than the Baltics to fight invasion. They also have a larger country and had a stronger military force. The Fins did, in fact, successfully defend themselves, and the Soviets were able only to occupy Finland's territory around Lake Ladoga.

The next day armed Communist tanks, military vehicles and soldiers appeared everywhere, even on the country roads. The red band on the left arm of some civilians, as well as tanks and other vehicles with red stars, became familiar sights to all of us. The radio carried the rules for living under the new regime. For the farmers, the first bad news was that they were now required to give the Soviets a certain share of their crops and animals. That announcement was an immediate challenge to the farmers, and they went to work figuring out how they could hide their livestock and crops from the Communist inspectors. All the farm families worked very hard to provide a decent life for themselves, and they were outraged that the Communists had imposed themselves upon Latvian life and wanted to steal from them.

About a week after the occupation I received a letter from my dad saying that many changes were taking place in the city, and that I should stay on the farm until school started. He said that he thought school would still be starting as usual, but that I was better off on the farm for now. I was fifteen and would be starting Technical School. In spite of all the trouble that had come to my country, I was eager to begin my new school, and I had a vague hope that soon things would somehow be better, and we'd go back to our normal lives.

We soon began hearing about other things that were changing in our country. From radio broadcasts we got the news that in place of the several radio stations we had, each broadcasting what they liked, there would now be only two authorized stations which would be controlled by the new Communist Government. We learned very soon that the only fare of those stations was Communist propaganda. Listening to any other radio transmissions would bring immediate punishment. We were also informed that unrestricted travel was outlawed. In order to leave our city or community, we must apply to the Communist government office and receive permission. Each new rule or change in our lives made our people more angry and fearful.

Each morning the farmers took their extra milk and butter to a collection and distribution center to sell what they didn't need. This was a place where the news was reported and passed around. Whoever took the milk in each day brought the news back to the farm. One day news was brought back that a number of our military officers from captain up were called to a special meeting by the Communists. As the days passed with no word from the missing officers, the families and everyone else became very apprehensive. Each day this was the topic of conversation on our farm and probably everyone else's. After about four weeks, word came that our men had been led into the forest and shot. We had all been hoping that they would appear with a reasonable explanation of why they had been detained so long. The news of their massacre sent waves of anger and terror throughout our people. Why had our men been shot when they and indeed our whole country had offered no resistance and were giving the invaders no trouble? Our military had laid down its arms, and the Russians had confiscated our weapons, our planes, and our one battleship and submarine. Our military strength had been very limited, and had mostly been used only for ceremonies and celebrations. Compared to the Communist military power, ours was almost laughable. We could not understand why our men had been shot for no reason when the Russians had easily taken control of our country already. We were forced to face the nature of our invaders and their murderous ways. There was no hope now that our lives might continue as before. We had a powerful, deadly enemy that was in control of our country and our lives. Fear prevailed.

In my young mind I was trying to sort it all out. What is communism? Why are they hurting us? What do they want with our country? Will my life change? Every day on the radio the speaker addressed us as "Comrades" and talked about equality, sacrifice and vision. I didn't understand any of it.

In spite of all that was happening, every day still had some pleasure. One day I was told by my uncle that I could take one of the horses to the blacksmith to have new shoes put on. I was very excited that I was trusted with this important task. I was thrilled watching the blacksmith do his exacting job, with the fire heating the metal so the shoe could be fitted to the horse. The blacksmith taught me how to hold the horse's leg so he wouldn't bolt and run away.

The women told me that before I returned to the city I must learn to milk a cow. It took quite a few tries, but I did it. It is not so simple as it might appear. The milker must gain the respect of the cow, for she punishes the amateur with a whipping by her tail or a kick.

In August, I went through the required "request to travel" procedure, and in a few days I was on my way home. I traveled on the train carrying a large smoked ham and big bags of rye and wheat flour for the work I had done that summer. This was my first payment for working. I was proud, and my parents were pleased that I was able to contribute needed food to our home.

5

At home, life was still pretty much the same, at least on the surface. Of course, our growing baby made some differences, but nothing to complain about.

One change in our lives was that food in the stores was rationed to us. Much of our food production was needed for the Red Army and their families. Meanwhile, my baby brother needed milk daily. I resumed my old job of going to the store. Now we had to stand in a long line for milk, and often it was gone before it was my turn. I began to notice that people were going into another nearby store and coming out with bags of food. On day I said to a man in my line, "Can I go to the other building to buy food and milk? Why are we standing here when other people are getting food quickly in the other store?" The man replied quietly, "No, no; that store is for party members and informers only. You should not ask questions."

I said, "But the radio says we are all comrades and everyone is equal."

He replied, "You must not say such things; you can get into serious trouble and your parents also." So I stood in line.

That evening when I told my parents about my experience, they looked at each other and my father said, "It is very sad that I must tell you this, but the man in the store is right. We no longer have the freedom to say what we want or to ask questions about the government. We must be careful what we say outside this house. There are people who would report you to the Communists if you say the wrong thing."

We were learning quickly that we had no recourse nor were we allowed to question anything that happened. In addition, my parents were beginning to understand that we couldn't be sure even of people we had known. We began to see that we had Communist collaborators among us, as some of those wearing the dreaded red arm band and the red star were fellow Latvians who had been part of the underground preparing for the invasion. I was stunned to see one of my elementary school teachers among them. It was estimated that five percent of Latvians were in this group of Communist supporters. We became cautious with everyone.

In our play field we began to see military troop training. We could not go to our familiar place until the soldiers were finished, so we liked to watch them until we could have the field. I had never seen a military person except our own soldiers in parades and walking on the streets. We all laughed at the Red Army soldiers because their uniforms were sloppy and they didn't look like real soldiers to us. The uniforms were a light gray-greenish color and the hats were made from the same material as the pants and had small visors. In the middle of the hat, it looked like somebody pushed a thumb through and covered it with fabric. Everybody was saying that the protrusions were for carrying their brains. The hats just looked ugly. Their boots were not leather, but canvas. Tucked in the top of their boots on the left side were a piece of newspaper and crude tobacco. Between exercises they would take out the newspaper, spread tobacco on it and roll it to make a cigarette. They would lick both ends to seal it, and then they lit and smoked. These horrible smelling "cigarettes" were called "mahorcas."

In their other boot they carried their eating utensils. We all thought they were very crude to eat with the utensils they had been sweating into all day. As teenagers do, we made fun of them to each other.

Another thing they did in rest periods was to run to the sea, take off their helmets, and stick their heads into the water to cool off. Then their helmets were put back on and they went back for more training. My dad, who had been a soldier in the Russian Revolution, also thought they were a little stupid for cooling off in salt water, as he said the salt water to the head combined with the perspiration under the helmet would lead to hair loss. We all thought that they were not very well trained or well equipped.

Many of the Red Army officers' families began to relocate to Latvia where the men were stationed. They were not welcome. My mother often talked with the neighborhood women, and I sometimes heard them talking about the Russian officers' wives. Our women made fun of them much as we ridiculed the soldiers. They said the wives must never have had anything nice, as they were buying every pretty thing in the stores even though they seemed not to know what to do with half of it. I remember one of the women saying that the Russian women were so unsophisticated they bought nightgowns to wear as formal dresses.

A terrible development was the Communists outlawing private ownership of property. We began to hear stories of Communist families deciding that they wanted to live in a certain house and the Latvian family being turned out of their own home without payment for the house or concern for the owner. Most of the Latvian people including my parents were paying on their homes as part of their retirement plan. My parents' three income-producing apartments were to be part of their old age security. Everyone was very frightened as they saw their friends losing everything they had worked for. The Communists also took whatever they wanted from the farms. Since the Communist party declared its ownership of everything, there was no security for anyone. Most of the farms had been in families for generations and the fact that the hard work of the family was not to secure the property for their children was heart breaking.

In the beginning the Russian soldiers and their families were objects of ridicule, but when we began to realize their power over us and the degree to which they would use that power, we no longer saw them as ridiculous or humorous, but terrifying. As for myself, as I began to understand what was happening, and as I became more mature, my rage at the Communists and my frustration at the unfairness of my country's plight became the root of a growing hatred toward our invaders.

Just before school started in early fall, a friend asked me if I'd like to make some money. He said, "We will go to the railroad station and there will be a pile of red beets that the farmers have delivered. Our job is to load the beets onto a railroad car so that they can be delivered to the sugar factory to be processed into sugar." For this we would each receive five lats. This job had to be done at night after the farmers had delivered the beets. It turned out to be much more work than we had thought. We used a large fork to pick up the beets from the ground and lift them into the railroad car. It was backbreaking work, but I was young and strong, and I was happy to earn the first money of my life. At this time, Latvian lats were being replaced by Russian rubles, so I lost almost all of the money in the exchange. My loss was very small, however, compared to some other people's almost total loss of their life savings. For instance, a bushel bag of devalued lats, which previously represented considerable wealth would now hardly buy a loaf of bread.

School started in September. One of our tenants worked for a Jewish tailor, and my mom engaged her to make a new school outfit for me: black wool pants and jacket. They fit perfectly. The uniform was the same as we had worn in elementary school, except for new school colors on our hats.

The first day of school was mostly ceremony and orientation. Each class had a class master, who acted as advisor and counselor. The principal announced that school would be much the same as before, except that the curriculum now included mandatory political science related to the Communist constitution and Russian language studies.

When elementary school started that fall, the children were encouraged by the new government to join the Pioneers, the children's branch of the Communist Party. They had special uniforms which were mandatory for party activities, and which could be worn to school also. Communist Party propaganda began early, and soon some children and teenagers were seen wearing the Communist uniform. Of course, many of the Russians who came into our country were already party members. Between the soldiers' families, our children who were coerced or seduced into party membership, and the families that had apparently, unknown to us, been underground Communists before the invasion, there were soon a number of Communist uniforms seen everywhere. It was said that acceptance into the University was dependent on Communist Party membership. Many of us hoped to attend the University. However, to my knowledge, none of my friends or neighbors joined the Party.

The political science class at my school was taught by a KGB officer in full Communist Party uniform. We were surprised that this person spoke Latvian fluently. We talked among ourselves and wondered why this was so. We heard that he had been born and raised in Latvia, and had later become a Communist. We could not figure out why, as we all felt very patriotic toward our own country, and could not imagine anyone changing his loyalty from Latvia to Communist Russia.

Regarding the school, it was difficult and much was required of us as students. The full course of attendance was five years. By the time we graduated we had to have completed another year's worth of hours working in various school approved machine shops. Actually, part of this requirement was met by our working four hours each on two days after regular school in a school-run shop where we learned the basics of using hand tools and machinery.

During the summers we were also required to work at least part-time as apprentices in school-approved manufacturing shops in the city, where we learned welding, foundry, and metal working, beginning with a file and chisel. By the time a student graduated from the Technical School he would be able to understand all aspects of manufacturing. We were given project specifications and were taught how to fulfill requirements. It was extremely painstaking work requiring attention to the most minute detail.

I was very thankful later in my life that I had learned so much in the school, although I was only able to complete three years of the course.

Most of our classes were as in any other school. We learned algebra, calculus, science, history, writing, etc. Our political science class was where we soon found a different attitude than we were used to. In the first couple of weeks a few of the boys in the class asked questions about the Communist constitution in a way that showed a preference for our previous independence. Questions were clearly not welcome, and were ignored as the instructor moved ahead in his lecture. Similar questions were in the mind of most of us, but we soon got the message that asking the questions was dangerous. We were not warned not to question what we were being taught but the lesson was not lost on us, as the boys who asked questions did not return to school. We found out later that they had been taken from their homes at night with no explanation. The threat of reprisal against dissenters and their families was very real. All of us learned fast to keep our mouths shut. I remembered what the man in the bread line had told me a few months before. The Communist method of rule by intimidation was in effect and was very effective.

One day at school I noticed an older boy, probably in his early twenties, wearing a leather coat. Most of the boys in our school liked to wear our uniform, but it was not mandatory. Someone told me his name was Konrads, and that he was the leader of an Aero Club in the city. He seemed interesting to me, as I was very attracted to aviation. When I first saw Konrads, I felt a strong desire to know him. Soon I stopped him in the hall.

"Is your name Konrads?" I asked.

"Yes. I am Konrads," he replied.

"I am so much interested in aviation, and I hear you are the leader of an Aero Club. Is it open for everyone, or can only certain persons belong?"

"The main requirement is a strong interest in aviation and the willingness to spend a lot of time working on gliders and learning about the principles of glider flying. We are glad to have new members if they meet these qualifications. Why don't you stop by our club one day soon and see what we are doing."

I could hardly wait and was very excited to see what the Aero Club was all about. The next Saturday I rushed to the building where it was located. The building belonged to the city, and I don't know how they got to use it, but it was perfect, like a big warehouse, and was full of aviation projects in progress. I was so happy to have made contact with people as involved in aviation as I wanted to be. I could hardly wait to tell my parents about it.

Konrads was the kind of person who always seemed to have ways to get what he needed or wanted. He had an old truck that was used to transport the gliders from the "warehouse" to the field where they would be flown. It would take two or three hours to get the gliders ready for transport to the field. By about 7 a.m. we wanted to start flying. I got up at 4 a.m. to begin the day's activities. Konrads was very much in charge of all the things connected with the club, and would not tolerate a minute's lateness, so I always made sure I got started very early. I should explain that these were not hand gliders like I was used to working on; these were real gliders that were large enough to hold a pilot.

The club members invited me to come around and help whenever I had time. I found time to be there often. My secret hope was that eventually I would be able to build and fly gliders.

One Sunday they invited me to come and work as one of the crew. I was filled with happiness and hope that I was being accepted as one of the group. Soon that wish came true, and I became a regular member of the club, and the aviation projects under way filled up my mind and all my free time.

Flying gliders requires skills, and much time was spent on learning how to fly from the ground up. It was a step-by-step and level-by-level process. We had experienced instructors giving us guidance for improvement. To qualify for the next level we needed our senior members' approval. The goal was to reach the third level. I didn't think anything could match the thrill of flying.

The Aero Club was the organization supported by the State and "Aisargi" during our independence years. Aisargi was composed of ex-military personnel from the army and air force and our president was their commander (similar to the National Guard in the U.S.). They had their own planes and flight school.

Years ago, in 1938, I remember headlines in our newspaper that one of the "Aisargi" flyers by the name of "Cukurs" would be flying to Gambia located in West Africa at the North Atlantic Ocean about 3,500 air miles from Riga (capital city of Latvia). According to our history, during Viking days some of our people were part of the explorers and discovered Gambia. It is a narrow strip of land rarely more than twenty kilometers wide which follows the river Koina; several tribes have their territories along the river. When the Atlantic Ocean was stormy the Vikings found the Koina River was a good place to dock their boats; and they claimed the river as their territory. I was surprised to learn from Alex Haley's "Roots" that the first slaves were brought to the U.S. from Gambia.

The pilot, Cukurs, took off in a single passenger, open-cockpit plane from Riga. He stayed along the river for several months, and his articles about his life there were published weekly in our newspaper. His return landing in my city's airport was an exciting day for us, and large crowds of people, including me, were gathered at the airport to give a great welcome to this returning pilot. It was so exciting to me to see the silver bird on the horizon and then approaching the landing strip. He made several circles above us, and the crowd was roaring and applauding. Now airplanes are so much a part of our daily lives, and we are so used to seeing them do all kinds of flying tricks in air shows, it's hard to imagine the great thrill of this crowd on the arrival of this pilot. Flying more than 3,500 air miles and doing circles in the air above us were not usual accomplishments. At that time, in that place, his feat was amazing and he was greatly admired as a hero.

After he landed, I tried to get as close as I could to see his face, his leather trousers and jacket, his pilot's hat and goggles. To this day I can still remember just how he looked and how I felt. To be a pilot seemed to me the most exciting thing in the world.

The Aisargi Pilots' Association was designing and building their own planes in the years before the Communist invasion. In Liepaja their facilities were the largest in the country. Konrads knew all the designers and pilots. He was planning to design and build a single engine airplane and he needed expert Aisargi consultation for design concepts. He studied book after book to learn technical aspects and the science of aerodynamics.

During the Russian occupation the number of Aisargi activities were limited, but the Pilots' Association still managed to continue most of their activities and gave full support to the Aero Club.

The purpose of the Aero Club was to give an opportunity for teenagers to participate and to develop skills to become glider pilots. The training program was according to European International regulations and standards. The most intensive glider training for teenagers was in Germany, and I speculate that they may have had an eye to future wars. An accomplishment award was a circular badge with dark blue background and silver wings. Three wings signified the highest level, and meant that a pilot was qualified for mother plane pull, which is the motor propelled airplane for pulling gliders into the air for high altitude solo piloting and the skill to find and control the thermal up-streams by performing thermal turns. A thermal uplift is the sun-ray-generated heat, reflected from different colored surfaces on earth which allow a pilot to continue flying for a longer period of time. The challenge was to find thermals which would extend the flight time. In the morning the first reflected sun ray heat could be found from light colored surfaces such as white sand on the beach. In the afternoon the heat is radiated by dark surfaces such as the forest. Finding thermals to give a lift to the glider prolonged flying time, and was the goal of glider pilots. In the club we had several people who wore three silver wings; they were our instructors. Konrads was the top leader of our group. After the Communists came, we feared day after day that they would find something wrong with what we were doing and would interrupt our activities. We were fortunate it didn't happen. However, we did hear one day that the KGB was looking for Konrads. As we hadn't seen him for several days this was bad news and we were afraid for him.

Konrads was living upstairs in his parents' home. His father was a furniture maker, and the house had a room addition on the back for his woodworking shop. We went to see his parents whom we knew pretty well. His mother opened the door and her face looked grim. She didn't seem to want to talk and only told us in a quiet voice that Konrads was not at home. We gathered from her attitude and words that something had happened to him. Cold chills started running through our bodies and we were silently questioning who would be next. For the next three or four weeks we heard nothing about Konrads. During that period war was declared between Germany and the Soviet Union. We knew that our country is between these two powers, so we were sure that there was more trouble ahead for us.

June 13, 1941, in the afternoon my dad brought from the garden house into our home a hand saw, an axe, a crowbar and some other hand tools. These he placed in a living room corner. My mom was packing some clothes for all of us. It was something unusual, but I didn't ask any questions. Sometimes my parents didn't tell me of frightening things going on, as they didn't want to alarm me. Later I found out that my dad somehow knew about a list of people who would be taken in the night, but didn't know if our names were on the list. My parents were preparing for the worst, in case we would be taken.

The next morning we learned that after midnight Soviet military vehicles with KGB members on board were roaring through the city. They had a list of individuals and families, who had only a few minutes to pack their things before they were taken. They were typically told in the middle of the night that they would be "settled elsewhere," and were taken to railway stations where they were herded into cattle cars with barred windows. About thirty thousand Latvian deportees who had left on very short notice with scant baggage were cut off from their homeland. There was no native language, no books, newspapers or schools. There was usually a severe lack of food and shelter. Many, possibly more than half, died of cold and hunger. Families were systematically torn apart. Men were sent to labor camps, from coal mines in Kazakhstan and Varkuta to lumber camps throughout Siberia. Women and children were taken to Siberian kolkhozes (community farms) and left to manage for themselves or to die. They built primitive huts for shelter, and dug up the hard ground to try to grow food; they had to try to survive until their poor crops ripened.We learned this through our grapevine of information from a few who escaped.

Who were these people whose names were on a list? School teachers, boy scout masters, factory workers, anyone, including our neighbor family on my street, whose father worked as a conductor for the city streetcar company. He was the one who amazed our neighborhood kids with his floating skill while reading the newspaper in the Baltic Sea. He taught me stamp collecting. His six children were my friends. That morning the house from the outside looked the same; I knocked and knocked on the door but nobody answered. They were all taken. What was their crime? No one knew.

There was a great sadness in the city because everyone knew someone whose name was on the list. June 14 was remembered as a "terror day" and Latvians still remember this day in churches and community centers in free countries with speeches and singing of the Latvian national anthem. Why, why all the suffering to our people? Was this genocide or a fear tactic to remind our people of the Communists' absolute power over us? I couldn't figure it out.

In later years, a few of the people who had been taken found their way back home to Latvia. These were so broken, emaciated and starved that they were not able to resume a normal life. Their families were destroyed, and so were they.

6

June was the month when summer was showing her beauty by returning leaves to trees, bringing bloom to flowers, and making everything feel fresh after the winter snow had been melted by the spring sun. We knew that summer was not far behind.

Our soccer field down the hill had new grass and was green from spring rains. The Baltic Sea was inviting everyone for summer activities. I was out of school, and my parents were planning for me to visit another farm in the country and help with farm work for a couple of months. This was the end of June, 1941, and we had been living under Communism for one year. The "terror day" was barely behind us. We were trying to go on with our lives as much as possible. I knew that the Germans, with military force, had taken over Poland and other countries but didn't pay much attention to what was going on all over Europe. I was a typical kid and had my own concerns and interests. Even if I had been more interested, the information available in my country was very limited. Radios and newspapers were controlled by the Communists.

One day I saw many people gathered by a "kioska" on a street corner. A kioska was a concrete tower, like a large post about four feet in diameter and eight feet tall with a roof. The kioska had a newspaper and magazine stand and reading benches. Every day newspapers and other entertainment news were glued on the side of a post. People passing by or waiting for a streetcar could stop and read, and young people used the kioska as a meeting place. As I was approaching the kioska I heard the word "war" several times. I asked an older man there, "Who will be fighting in this war everyone is talking about?"

He replied, "Only the Germans and Russians are actually at war, but the trouble is, we are caught in the middle between them."

I didn't see any expression on his face or on the faces of the people he was talking to about the war. I think they had learned already that it was better not to show your feelings when living under the Communists.

I rushed home to tell my dad what I had heard, but I was too late; he already knew about the war. That day it was not hard to tell that something had happened; there was much more air activity than usual. Large numbers of Russian fighter planes, MIG-12's and YAK-9's were in the air spoiling the peaceful day.

My dad told me to get a shovel, hammer, nails, and wood planks that were stored along our garden house for drying. He said, "We are going to build a bunker."

We walked across the street to the open field with sandy hills behind our potato field and vegetable garden. A picket fence separated the field from the street, and lots of flowers, including sunflowers, were growing behind the fence. The field was about eighty feet deep. At the end of the field was a deep water well, which was used for the vegetable garden. My street was short, having only six houses, and these were only on one side of it. At one end there was a small grocery store, and on the main street joining mine, there was a streetcar stop. My street was a dead end, with weeping willows along it for protection from winter winds that would carry snow onto the street.

We walked to the sandy hill, and my dad chose a spot where we would be digging and building the bunker. My dad said, "We don't know what will happen when the Germans and Russians start fighting, but some of it will no doubt be in our country. Staying in the house would be very dangerous if it should be hit by mortar shells or a bomb from the air. Or Russians could use our house as a hiding place. Living so near the Baltic Sea makes our house a target, as many Russian military are in the immediate area."

After clearing the spot for the bunker, we went back to the house and gathered our three renters. They were all afraid for their families just as my parents were. My dad and the others agreed to help digging and setting up wood planks so that the walls and ceiling wouldn't cave in. The sand thickness should be enough so that bullets couldn't penetrate. My dad had been in the Czar's army during the Russian Revolution and he knew how to build a bunker. With all the help we had, a bunker large enough to accommodate four families was built in one and a half days. My mother prepared containers with food and drinking water, which we carried to the bunker. We took kerosene lamps, lots of blankets and whatever else we would need for an emergency.

Neighbors on our street noticed the pile of sand that we were digging and were curious about what we were doing. After talking to us, they went home and started looking for shovels and building materials.

The weather was beautiful, but I was afraid to go to the beach or any other place. We all stayed at home together. We had agreed that if we started hearing artillery shelling or having air strikes we would run as fast as we could to the bunker. It was very frightening, but of course we were somewhat used to being afraid after the Communist invasion only a year ago. How could it be happening to us again?

There was not any news on the radio or newspapers about the war. We had to let our own experience and instincts dictate what we should do. Because of our history we didn't have any sympathy for the Germans. For several hundred years our people had lived under German feudalism, where they were like slaves, taking care of the baron's land, raising crops and animals, and working from sun-up to sun-down for only a small parcel of land. They were able to work their own land only after all the baron's work was done. Many of our folk songs reflect the sadness and futility of that time.

After the war I read an article in a magazine that said that all German-conquered countries would have been divided up and the land assigned to German officers to belong to their families. This was not accomplished, as the Germans did not win the war. If they had won, it is likely that the Baltics and other countries would be under feudalism similar to that endured by our ancestors.

During the time we were sitting in our house, knowing we had a safe haven (our bunker) my parents were quietly waiting most of the time, but when they did talk, I could tell they felt both hopeful and afraid. We all hated the Communists, so in some ways, Germans in our country seemed an improvement, but on the other hand, we all knew our history as slaves of the Germans, and we prayed that they had changed and would not enslave our people again.

I remembered the summer before when my country had been occupied by the Red Army, and the terrifying year we had lived under their rule. I remembered Konrads and other friends who had just disappeared, those we could not even ask about. Cold chills went down my spine, and I said to myself, "What can be worse than living under Communism?" I tried to be optimistic, as did my countrymen; maybe the Germans would be our liberators. I thought then that I would do everything I could to get as far as possible from the Communists.

Two days after the bunker was built, the silence was broken, and we could hear artillery guns firing some distance away; it was time to go to the bunker. It was actually quite cozy living in close quarters. Men started playing cards and the women were knitting or talking and the kids most of the day were playing outside the bunker, being careful to stay close to our temporary home. A couple of times when my mom needed something from the house I was sent back when the shelling was quiet to get it. I was only crossing our potato field, but I ran as fast as I could. Any time we heard artillery shelling or planes overhead, the men stopped playing cards and tried to figure out how far the German tanks were from our city.

During the first two days playing outside the bunker, I could see Red Army tanks moving along the Baltic Sea, and on our main street motorized vehicles with the red star pulling heavy guns and other military equipment. I didn't know if they were going or coming, but I knew it was a real war.

During the night I didn't get much sleep as it was very noisy and scary. Airplanes were flying, anti-aircraft and anti-tank guns were firing and tanks and military vehicles were moving close to our bunker.

Before daybreak, the noise disappeared, and it was quiet. Only a few gunshots could be heard. We knew the Germans were coming.

When there was enough daylight, I peeked through the bunker to see who was walking in our neighborhood. I was surprised to see several dozen Red Army foot soldiers walking through the trees and shrubs along the Baltic Sea. It looked to me that they were disoriented and didn't know where they were going. I think they were separated from their troops because of the fighting.

That morning the sun was shining its promise for another nice day. The water in the Baltic Sea was blue, and only a few ripples could be seen on the surface. If I could have it my way, I would be at the sea swimming, and there would be no war to worry about. I longed for the happy days before last year, when this nightmare began. I had good parents, though, who were concerned about me and they didn't even want me to go out of the bunker that morning. It took awhile to convince them that I would be only a few feet away.

I remembered times when I was waiting for the sun to disappear over the horizon of the Baltic Sea. When I looked there from my home I was looking west. Now I was outside on top of the bunker and when I was looking southwest I could see fairly flat uncultivated land with some grass, shrubs, and in some areas just white sand. Further south I could ordinarily see our main street and streetcar stop. But that morning there were no streetcars on the street or fishing boats in the sea. Looking further down the street, I could see the lard manufacturing plant and warehouse on the other side. Every time I looked at the lard factory it reminded me of times when I was younger and waiting for ships to arrive in our harbor near my house with their coconut cargo. In addition to my friends and I having so much fun picking up the coconuts from broken sacks, we also liked to watch the pallets full of sacks that were lifted from the ship cargo bay, lowered onto a truck bed and taken to the lard factory. There the lard was made and packed in approximately ten-pound barrels for distribution to the stores. Most of the food store items were carried in bulk and customers had their own containers.

In our climate, coconut palms didn't grow. Our weather was too cold during winter, and the summer was too short. During the winter months from September to February the average temperature was very low and snow from two to four feet was on the ground all winter, until it started melting in the beginning of May.

That morning I didn't have much inspiration to participate in games when I was outside the bunker. I just stood there and looked at my home with its white picket fence, potato fields, and the graceful sunflowers surrounding our garden house, wondering how those flowers follow the sun all day by twisting their long stems. I turned my head to the open field and looked at shrubs some distance away and all of a sudden couldn't believe what I was seeing; four soldiers emerged from behind a bush and started walking. I froze, afraid, but my curiosity overcame my fear. I looked at them for several seconds. I believed they saw me, but didn't perceive me as much of a threat. They had noticed our bunker, and started walking toward it. I turned my head to the left and right and there were more of them. I knew they were Germans. I turned around and dived into the bunker hole like a prairie dog. I was so tense and frightened, all I could say was "Germans." Everybody knew the meaning of that word and sat very quietly for a few long minutes, wondering what would happen next. I noticed moving shadows from the bunker entrance opening. I raised my eyes to the opening and there were boots and uniforms and machine guns pointing at us. My heart started pounding.

They said something in their language, but we didn't understand. The soldiers used their flashlight to check out our bunker; then they left. By the presence of German soldiers we were terrified, but after they left, smiles returned to all our faces and everybody started talking at the same time. We were so frightened by what had been happening in our country and by all the people who had disappeared, I guess we were afraid we'd all be shot on the spot. We had no idea what to expect from these new occupiers of our country.

We stayed in the bunker. When I peered through the opening I could see a continuous flow of German motorized military vehicles on Main Street, moving east.

Machine gun rounds were heard for some time. I was so thankful for my dad's wisdom in building the bunker. When the shooting was loud and close I was feeling safe surrounded by the wood planks and the pile of dirt and sand.

About three hours later German soldiers came back and scared us again, waving us to come out from the bunker and to go in the direction they pointed -- towards the lard factory. At that time, about twenty street residents were ordered out of their homes and hiding places and were also sent in the same direction. The street section along the lard factory and warehouse was closed, and military traffic was detoured through other streets.

We followed the crowd, and soon more than eight hundred people were packed into that small section. German soldiers with rolled-up shirt sleeves and machine guns were at each end of the street section so that nobody could get out. My dad told me that German soldiers were searching the area for hiding Red Army soldiers and guns. About two hours later they told us to go home. What a relief we felt! We moved home from the bunker.

In one day's time the hands of authority in our city were changed from Russian to German. It was nice to be home, but a black cloud of uncertainty hung over our heads.

7

On April 24th of 1941 I had become sixteen years old. My present was a used sports bike in very good working condition. Particularly I liked the wooden rims painted yellow and the bent-down handles. I had wanted a bike like that for a long time, and I was thrilled to get it. I took it to show to my friends, and they all tried it out and liked it too. The next day I waxed and lubricated it, and tightened all the nuts and bolts; it was in tip-top condition. I chose a special storage place for it in our garden house.

This bike was very special to me, though I had had bikes before. My previous ones were old and not in good condition. They seemed to be always broken down and I spent a lot of time fixing them. Maybe I was too rough riding them. Dad and mom had bikes and before my brother was born we took long rides on country roads. My mom would make sandwiches and other good things for a picnic. Everything tasted so good after riding in that fresh country air. Biking was one of my favorite outings.

The main street in my neighborhood was one where military motorized German units were moving their forces. One day in July, I was standing at the street corner with my bike watching passing big and small trucks and motorcycle units. At the end of these vehicles were soldiers riding bicycles. I could have been watching a parade, but realized the horrible truth -- that this was for real. All these vehicles and men were invading our country. Suddenly, one of the soldiers jumped out of the line and came toward me. I soon realized what he wanted as he threw down his clunker bike, grabbed my beautiful bike and went riding off on it. I couldn't believe that the bike I loved so much was gone. In spite of my age, I began crying in frustration, and ran home to tell my parents what had happened. Once again we were reminded of what little control we had over our own lives. I know my parents were very sad at my loss and disappoint-ment, but they were helpless. They were understanding as I used all the bad words I could think of in hatred of the Germans. We realized that even though the Communists were gone, we had another monkey on our backs. The Germans had taken over our whole country in about a week.

A few days after my city, Liepaja, was taken, we found out a little more about battles in the vicinity. I was born and raised in this city. Riga is our capital city and the largest. Liepaja was the second largest and very unique with architecture influenced by the Swedish, Polish, Germans and Russians, all of whom at one time or another had governed my country.

Many years before, a large canal was built to connect the Baltic Sea with a large lake. The canal was built wide and deep to accommodate international ships for imports and exports. Ships were docked at one side of the canal, and warehouses were built on the same side. Along the canal there was action all the time. That was the place where I used to pick up used lead seals for New Year's Eve and got a hard spanking from my dad for spending too much time by the canal.

The two-way wide bridge crossed the canal and divided the city into Old Town and New Town. I lived in the part called New Town. My elementary school and airfield where my flying activities took place were also on that side of town. However, the Technical School and Aero Club were on the Old Town side. On the opposite side of the bridge from the big ships, commercial fishing and pleasure boats were docked; by going under the bridge, they could enter into the sea. Close to the lake was the Yacht Club; sailing was very popular in the lake.

The most common transportation was streetcars. They looked much like those in San Francisco today. There were not many automobiles on the streets but lots of horses and wagons. Farmers brought farm products to the stores and bought what they needed. The people who wanted to go "with class" took a horse and carriage; the driver was dressed in black tails and wore a high black hat.

We had many parks and lots of trees along the streets with flowers everywhere. I especially liked the parks with gazebos, lakes, and white swans swimming. Many Sundays I went to the park to hear my dad playing in the Police Department band. Those were the good old days.

We heard of five battles in the vicinity of the city where the Red Army, in June, 1941, gave resistance. However, the German panther tanks with grenadiers (soldiers) aboard and the Luftwaffes' superiority overwhelmed the Russians in a short time. They left burned and damaged tanks and other war machinery on roads and fields all around our city. There was considerable damage. The Red Army was running and took Communists from Latvia with them. They only left behind their burned out tanks with the red star. The tanks left on the road were pushed aside by the Germans. They did not add to the beauty of our cities. The Germans were moving their military force east to invade Russia.

There was an immediate need to establish a new city, county, and state government who would try to resist German demands as much as possible and try to negotiate to our people's advantage.

Immediately after the first day of the occupation, the Germans demanded food supplies for their army.

It was known that in other occupied countries, the Germans drafted the local men to help execute Hitler's plan. We were expecting that the German draft would be inflicted on us. We didn't know what the future would be, but smiles started returning and people started talking to each other, even though their voices were filled with sadness as they talked about relatives and friends they had lost during the Communist occupation. At least under the Germans, we were free to talk after having our lips tight for a year. Children were allowed to listen when their parents were talking. There had been cases under the Communists where parents were taken from their homes, never to be seen again, because of their children innocently repeating talk they had heard around home. Whether justified or not, some happiness was felt in the air as we saw the Communists go.

The biggest excitement to me was the news that Konrads was alive and would be home in a few days. My feeling was that Konrads wouldn't be himself if he couldn't return from the dead. I admired him so much. When we got together again, he explained what had happened. He knew that the KGB was looking for him, but had managed to slip away several times with his parents' help. He knew that there were limits to how much longer they would tolerate not being able to find him; it could be real trouble for his parents. He expected that the next time they could come during the night.

Sometime before that I had needed a book and went to see Konrads to find out if he had what I was looking for. He showed me his room upstairs in his parents' house. In his room was a bed, dresser, closet, bookshelves, big table, and in the corner, a wood airplane propeller. The table top was covered with glass over a world map. He said his dream was to design and build his own airplane and to fly around the world. It was very exciting to me to hear such talk. His window was facing the back yard that was large and filled with fruit trees, red and black berry bushes, vegetables, and flowers. A high fence surrounded the property, and the main entrance gate to the back yard was located at the side of the house where the addition was built for his dad's woodworking shop. Outside the building were stacks of lumber under a roof for drying and use in furniture making. On the far side of the back yard was a smaller gate allowing entrance into the back yard from the other street.

Under the mat at the back door entrance he placed several flat electrical switches, low voltage, and battery operated. From one of his bedroom 220 volt electrical circuits he disconnected the wires from the circuit breaker. The circuit breaker box was in the basement. He said that from the floor mat it was easy to run small wires through cracks into the basement and to connect them to the wires that he had disconnected from the bedroom circuit breaker. Wires and connections were invisible in the basement. In the electrical outlet close to his bed he plugged in a small electrical beeper. Any time someone stepped on the front door floor mat, the beeper made a warning sound in his bedroom. On a window casing facing the back yard he bolted a piece of wood to the window upper jamb and painted it so it looked like part of the window. Small cuts were made in the piece of wood so a rope hook could be attached to it. Above the rope hook about four inches was a painted nail projecting out about one-eighth of an inch. Fishing line was attached to the rope hook and placed over the nail. When the window was open he could grab the rope and lower himself so that he could close the window, and in a few seconds he was down to the ground. He pulled the fishing line after himself and separated the rope hook from the piece of wood, and the rope was free to fall to the ground. The beeper he had pulled out from the electric outlet before he opened the window and it was in his pocket. There was nothing left behind to reveal his actions nor to incriminate his parents. Konrads was an athletic guy, and he practiced his escape several times until he could get out and down in ten seconds. His motorcycle was parked in his back yard close to the small gate that was far from his house.

He was right in his predictions. He related what had happened. One night after midnight his beeper went off and he knew what he must do. When he was on the ground, he folded the rope and ran with it to his motorcycle and placed it in the motorcycle bag with some books that were there. The small gate was leading to another street far from his house. He left the city and was heading for his uncle's farm in the country. On the way to the farm he was thinking about his parents. The plan he had executed was kept secret from them. They knew nothing of his escape plan. He felt it was safer for them if they didn't know how he escaped or where he was heading. He was sure the KGB would be questioning them and searching the house. He believed in our old saying, "Eyes are talking when a person is lying." He didn't leave behind any clues. He knew his parents would be very worried to find him gone, but it was better than to have them worry after the KGB took him.

Close to his uncle's farm was a forest, where he left his motorcycle; he walked to the farm house. He needed to talk to his uncle. He waited awhile until his uncle came out of the house and headed toward the horses in the meadow. His uncle was surprised to see him. Konrads explained, "I need a place to stay and hide out for awhile. Of course, I don't want to endanger your family, so no one must know I'm here. I would appreciate some food if you can spare a little, and please place it by this rock pile on the edge of the forest."

His uncle replied that he would be glad to help however he could. They shook hands and parted, the farmer to his chores and Konrads to his forest hideout. Everything was there that he needed to survive, and he felt fortunate that it was not winter and that he was not in a Russian labor camp.

Dry branches were his bed; red, black, and blueberries were a supplement to the food his uncle brought, and there were streams for drinking water and for bathing. The first thing he needed was sleep, so he lay down. He couldn't sleep for awhile, and his mind was going over what he had done, and worrying about his parents finding him gone. The cheerful forest sounds eventually sang him to sleep. A few days later, after exploring the forest around him and getting things organized, he felt much better, and began reading a book that was in his bag, "How to Build an Airplane."

Luck was on his side and after he was four weeks in the forest, Germany proclaimed war with Russia. That was in July 1941, and in a couple of weeks the Russians were out, and the Germans were in. One day his uncle left a note with his food. "Come home; the Communists and KGB are gone, and there are no more Russians in our country." Konrads couldn't believe what had happened in the four weeks he had been living in the woods. He visited his uncle's family for a few days, but was anxious to get home and relieve his parents' worry about what had happened to him.

He said, "My heart was pounding as I tried to find a door key. My mother heard me and opened the door with a big smile and hug. She was so happy to find out that I was all right. I was very happy, too, that our family was together again and all unharmed."

His parents told him that on the night he left, KGB agents had been at the door and had questioned his parents and searched the house. His parents were very worried about him, and were afraid the KGB would come back again and again. They were terrified that he had been found and they would never see him again. They were afraid every time they heard a knock on the door. The KGB never came back. This, of itself, was very frightening in a way, as his parents feared that the reason the KGB didn't return was that they had found Konrads. A likely explanation for the failure of the KGB to return is that at that time the Germans were beginning to give the Communists serious trouble, and the Russians no longer were focused on the Latvians, but on their own survival. They were probably concentrating on fleeing back to Russia.

Konrads' story was inspirational to all of us, but made us realize again how close we all were to danger under the Communists. Konrads being back gave direction to my life. He was a great influence on me.

In the city, life was going on, and some noticeable changes were taking place. During the Russian occupation, the Latvian lat was replaced by the Russian ruble, and now was changed to the German mark. Stores were almost empty, and there was very little to buy. The exchange rate between rubles and marks was so great that those who had managed the Russian occupation without financial ruin lost everything now.

Food rationing continued, but with new books being issued to be stamped at each purchase. Almost everything that was not rationed was raised by my dad. His garden continued to provide a great part of our diet.

It is interesting that Germany and Russia demanded so much from our farmers, yet the farmers managed not only to survive but to live fairly well. During the German occupation they were better off than the people in the city. They had something that everybody wanted. Not only did the invaders want farm products, but city people were hungry for good bacon, eggs, steak, and other things from the farm. The farmers had learned during the previous year to cheat and pay off inspectors, to hide and raise animals in the forest, and to satisfy the demands of an occupational government. They realized the importance of having adequate records and staying in the good graces of the invaders, but they managed also to take care of themselves.

All conditions were right for a black market; the money that was available had very little value. An exchange system informally started in which goods and services were exchanged. Bacon became the exchange value. For a slab of bacon of about five pounds you could buy a good suit. For a pig, farmers could obtain copper wire and hardware to install electricity on their farms. At that time many farmers were still using kerosene lamps; copper wire on the Latvian market was too expensive for the farmers to buy. The Germans wanted bacon and they had seemingly limitless access to copper wire. During the German occupation almost all farms had electricity installed.

Two or three elementary schools in the city were taken over by the Germans to establish military hospitals. When it was time for the elementary schools to start in September, many students discovered that they didn't have a school to go to. Other schools became overcrowded. Several high schools and large buildings were taken over by the military and associated civilians.

Not far from my home was an open field, and I noticed that some work was going on in that area. Simple structure barracks were set up by the dozens, and high barbed wire fences were built around the area with observation towers. I wondered what it was, so I asked. I was told it was a prison camp, and that they were building more in the vicinity. During the couple of years after the German occupation, we began to hear and see what was going on in these prisons. If we had any illusions about the Germans, we lost them then; the way the Germans treated their prisoners was very inhumane. Sometimes in winter when it was bitter cold outside, we saw "escorted" prisoners walking in our streets. They had no shoes, but potato sacks were wrapped around their feet and bodies in a futile effort to find some warmth. They looked like bundles of rags moving slowly in our streets. The sight of their cold feet and emaciated bodies made my friends and I very sad, even though many of the prisoners were the hated Russians. The sight of them made us fear the Germans even more than ever.

Increasing numbers of German soldiers were noticeable on our streets. The airfield that we were using for flying gliders was occupied by the German Luftwaffe, with several dozen ME-109 and F-190 fighter planes stationed there. During the period when changes were taking place, our Aero Club activities were suspended for awhile. This was also the period when Konrads was gone. When he returned, the next day he was back to the Aero Club in the warehouse trying to figure out how he could air-cool his four-cylinder short block Ford engine that he was planning to use for his airplane in progress. The engine was purchased, with his friends' help, from England, and was the best one he could afford. It was set on a stand and ran very well, but it was water-cooled. This required a radiator and liquid coolant circulating through the engine block and head. He knew that conversions from water to air cooled engines were made in England and Germany, so it could be done. For air cooling he needed aluminum alloy finned engine head (like on a motorcycle now.) Fins were needed to increase the surface area to have a better heat dissipation. He knew all the advantages of an air-cooled engine: simplified fuselage design, reliability and weight reduction. These goals were very desirable to achieve. The problem was that aluminum alloy was very difficult to cast at that time. Aluminum melting point and solidification point are very close together. The metal didn't have enough time to complete the flow in a mold to form a part before it became solid. The mold needed to be pre-heated and that's where the complication started. Technology was not as advanced as now. Knowing the difficulties to cast an engine head didn't stop Konrads from achieving it. He went to the library and got all the books and publications that were available about aluminum casting -- even books in German that he translated into Latvian using his little knowledge of German and a dictionary. Konrads knew all the machine shops and foundries in town. A big help was his dad's woodworking shop where he made a fine grain birch wood pattern for a mold. After about a year of making several changes in his approach, he was successful and very proud to have an aluminum cast engine head. He had learned how to pre-heat the mold and control the temperature, so the metal wouldn't solidify too soon. It was quite an accomplishment.

In our minds we were questioning where we would be able to fly our gliders. This problem was presented to city officials and cleared with German authorities. The answer was positive that we could use the airfield, but we had to submit all names of active members to the airfield (now military) "commandant" who was in charge of operations; every morning when we arrived we must contact him with information about that day's activities. We said, "Fair enough," and we were flying again.

Technical School started in the middle of September and the curriculum was the same as prior to the Russian occupation. We were happy to be relieved of Communist political science and Russian language study. The Germans did not interfere with our regular education.

8

Soon after school started we got snow; at the beginning of October we had a foot of it on the ground. I waxed my skis and decided to try the hills close to the airport. Tall pine trees were growing there and made skiing more interesting. There were a number of skiers and kids with sleds.

On a flat area next to the hill I noticed a metal fence built along the hillside. This fence wasn't there last year. Further down on the flat area heavy equipment and large boxes were stored. Closer to our skiing place were two airplanes. A German soldier guard was patrolling the area, walking back and forth along the equipment stored there. Those two planes looked like very lonely sitting ducks. I started skiing closer and closer. I noticed a red star on each plane. Both were the same; two seaters, open cockpits with five star radial engines. Radial engine cylinders are located parallel with the propeller, and the number of cylinders is always uneven. I recognized the planes as Russian Air Force U-2 pilot training planes. I touched them several times and decided to get inside the cockpit. I thought if the German guard noticed me and didn't like my presence he would tell me, "Go away" and I would. When I got inside the plane I liked everything I saw: open cockpit, windshield, instrument panel, and comfortable seats. It looked to me like it was in good working condition.

This airport had been used by the Russian Air Force, with all different types of military aircraft flying in and out, including MIG-12's and YAK's. After the German invasion there were not any military aircraft left on the ground with the exception of these two trainer planes. Maybe the Red Army didn't have enough pilots available when they were running from the Germans.

I could see the engine starter button, and all I had to do was just put my finger on it and push. At the last second I decided it might not be wise to do that. If the engine started it might be too much for the German guard to take, and I didn't know how to stop the engine once I got it started. I got out of the plane and opened the engine compartment. It was so easy to do I didn't need any tools. I liked, I really liked that engine very much. It was air-cooled with aluminum heads; the size of the five cylinders was approximately three feet in diameter. I studied the engine support three-point mounting arrangement with mounting bolts passing through heavy rubber absorbers to minimize vibration. Magneto type engine ignition and starter were used with a double fuel line system for redundancy. This plane was small but had advanced features in design.

I spent at least an hour around there without being interrupted by the German guard. I came to the conclusion that the Germans might not have much interest in the Russian planes, but I wanted to explore these thoughts a little more at some other time. I had an idea in my head, but I kept it secret and told no one. During the night I was thinking about that engine and navigational instruments in the cockpit control panel. I had a dream of flying that plane.

A couple of days later I put some tools in my pocket: a screwdriver, small open socket wrenches, and cutting pliers. I put my skis on and went back to the hill. There was always somebody skiing. I skied for a little while and didn't see any changes around the planes. The German guard was still walking back and forth around the heavy equipment. I skied to the plane and opened the engine compartment; without any second thoughts I started cutting the engine mount and fuel line safety wires that were used to guarantee reliability. That mounting hardware never would vibrate loose. Special bolts and nuts were used in the aircraft industry. Bolts were pre-drilled with small holes, and hexagonal crown nails were drilled across the corners. After the nuts were torqued, a small metal wire was inserted into the bolt hole and through the hexagonal nut hole in a clockwise direction and twisted.

I knew that I was committing a crime. I tried to rationalize what I was doing by thinking that this is a Russian plane, and what would the Germans do with it anyway? They do not have operational, service or maintenance manuals or spare parts or trained pilots for it. Eventually they (Germans) will scrap that plane and it will end up in a junk yard. After these thoughts I felt better, and pulled out a right-sized wrench for the engine mount nuts. In a short time all three nuts were loose, and the bolts could be pulled out easily. I left the nuts on the end of the bolts, and only two more fuel line nuts were needed to break it loose. I cut electrical wires leaving connectors on the engine side. The engine with propeller was ready to be separated from the fuselage struts (supports.) I closed the engine compartment, and went back to the hill skiing. I stayed for another hour. I watched the German guard, and he was still walking back and forth. For the next week I was undecided and worried whether to reveal my secret thought: to steal the Red Army Air Force plane engine, guarded by the German soldiers. I never stole anything in my life. I was a policeman's son, and I could never tell my dad what I was thinking of doing. Why I had such a compulsion to steal that engine I couldn't understand myself. I needed the help of at least two more men to take the engine out of the plane. I didn't have any need for that engine but I was thinking about the Aero Club. This might be a lifetime opportunity to have such an engine in our hands. Maybe Konrads could use it for his plane, or maybe some other club member with his expertise could design and build his own plane. My final decision, for whatever reason, was -- I had to do it or die trying.

I contacted two club members, and the first words they said were, "Are you crazy?" After I gave more details and explained my plan, they agreed; we had to do it.

The plan was to get a long, heavy-duty sled and several white sheets and then wait till it started snowing. It was a text-book operation and took less than ten minutes to lower the engine onto the sled and cover it with the white sheets. I looked in the direction where heavy machinery was stored, and the German soldier guard was still walking. One of us pulled the sled and two others were skiing on each side of it. After awhile we changed.

Konrads and the other club members couldn't believe what we had done. They all agreed that there might never be another opportunity to have such a good engine in our hands. We didn't feel too guilty stealing from the Germans or Russians. They had both stolen our country.

Konrads looked and looked at our engine, and concluded that too many changes would be required to incorporate this engine into the plane he was building. However, for future plane design the engine would be very desirable. All three of us felt that we had done something good for the club. The first step would be to set it up on a wood support stand and try to get it started. We could learn thrust output by measuring force at different throttle positions. This information was very important for future plane design. I slept well that night.

The same lady who made my new school uniform was willing to make a winter coat for me from my dad's police uniform coat. The material was light gray and heavy. I had the style that I wanted in my mind including a partial belt sewn permanently to the back, large outside pockets with flaps, and a nice slippery lining. She said, "I have to take the coat apart to see if there is enough material to do all of that." I said, laughing, "Please stretch it." A couple of days later she said that there was enough material for the coat I wanted. She was the wife of a man who worked in the lard factory making wood barrels. They didn't have any children, and she seemed to especially like me. The coat turned out to be exactly what I wanted.

My dad said he had an extra pair of leather boots, and he thought maybe I was big enough now to fit them. He didn't have to ask me twice to try them. I slipped my foot into the boot, and it was just right for me. I felt that I was a big boy then, able to wear my dad's boots. Like most children, I was anxious to grow up. During the winter months I was proudly wearing my new coat, boots, and my hat with school colors.

One day Konrads told me that he was seeing a nice girl, and she had a good looking younger sister. He asked me if I would be interested in meeting her and having a double date. I told him I had never dated a girl before and wouldn't know what to do. He said that we would all be going together, maybe to the movies or something similar. Whatever Konrads said was fine with me. We ended up going to the movies. I was very nervous from the beginning and didn't know what to say. We were sitting close on theater seats, and her charm, quiet voice and perfume put me in heaven. After the movie was over, I didn't remember much of it, but I started feeling attracted to the female presence. Most of all, it was my first date, and I was feeling good about it. I met her several other times, going to the gymnasium she attended. I liked her very much, but that was as far as I wanted it to go.

Girls felt that the boys wearing the green hats were special because we didn't have girls in our school. Often we received invitations to attend their social activities, such as dances and stage performances carried out in their gymnasium main auditorium.

One day in the warehouse where club activities took place we came to the conclusion that we couldn't work all the time, and we needed some other fun too. We decided to have a party and invite the girls from gymnasium. We had to limit the number of invitations; otherwise all the gymnasium girls would come. We chose two classes to invite, about twenty-five girls. Later on we heard that the boys from those classes didn't like us; they thought we were stealing their girls.

In the warehouse we had several partitioned rooms and we cleared out one of them. Loudspeakers were installed, and a good record player was brought with our favorite records for dancing. The room was decorated with large hand-painted pictures, including some of our favorite airplanes. Freshly cut pine tree branches were stretched along the wall to give their nice aroma for the party. Special lighting effects were provided by using a high powered light dimmer and different colored light filters. Chairs were set along the walls, and several tables held snacks and finger foods.

Boys wouldn't be boys, especially in this group, if they didn't dream up something special. Our chairs were made of wood; two nails were driven into the seats of six of them. The nail heads were barely visible on top of the chair seat, and on the bottom projected about half an inch. Small wires were soldered to the nail projection on the seat bottoms, and wires were passed through the wall to the other side. The wires were connected to three magnetos. The magnetos' legitimate use was for aircraft internal combustion engines as an alternator to generate current for ignition. We had about a dozen of them for club use, given to us by the Aisargi organization. Three magnetos were modified by attaching handles to the shafts. By giving a kick with the handle, a high voltage pulse was generated. If someone touched these two wires or nail heads, the high voltage would discharge through the body and a person would feel a slight shock, similar to touching a spark plug wire with the engine running. This of course happened when someone sat in one of the wired chairs.

Girls started arriving two or more at a time. They were all beautifully dressed, and their hair was arranged for a party. No make-up, no nail polish, just natural beauty, and I liked them all.

We invited twenty-five and they all came. After introductions all round, the party was begun with a waltz. I was so excited, although my dancing was not that great. I had had some dance lessons in my physical education classes, but I didn't have much experience. A few times I stepped on a girl's toes, but after apologies, they forgave me.

In our crowd, new talents were always being discovered; some boys were able to tell jokes and make a crowd laugh. Singing the songs we all knew soon established friendships, and we all felt comfortable. Everybody was having a great time.

Nobody in our club smoked cigarettes or drank hard liquor. I think one of the reasons for our abstinence was that all the club members were hoping to become pilots, and we all knew that physical requirements and competition for acceptance to Pilots' School were very high. Therefore, we tried to eliminate anything that would alter our minds or dull our senses. We couldn't have asked for a better party without smoking or drinking liquor.

The culmination of the party was the boys' game. We all knew which were the six chairs with nails in the seats, and we avoided sitting on them. Between dances these "special chairs" were occupied by girls, and three boys went into the back room and sequentially started kicking the magneto handles.   The effect was all we had hoped for. We were all talking and suddenly one girl got up from her chair with a surprised grin on her face; she turned around and looked at the chair, then touched it with her hand and couldn't find anything unusual.   She said she felt like she was stung by a bee.   We didn't say anything, and soon the five girls in the other wired chairs started jumping up the same way.   The boys started laughing and clapping their hands and shouting, "It worked."   Girls jumped in the boys' laps and said, "Just wait; we'll dream up something better for revenge."   It was just one big laugh, and the next day all the gymnasium knew about the artificial bee stings.

I started getting the feeling of being a teenager, but it didn't last long.

One day the newspaper had a headline; the German Army wanted our young men from ages eighteen to twenty-five for the first draft.   We were expecting and dreading that this would happen, because they had issued draft orders in the other countries they had invaded.   Registration centers were established, and notification papers were sent to those who were affected.   There was only a very slim chance of avoiding the draft.   Almost everybody eligible had to go.   It didn't matter who you knew or how much bacon you had.   Only if a person could prove that he was mentally retarded or physically unfit to serve could he be exempt.   The Germans didn't trust Latvian doctors' statements about a disability, and they reviewed each case themselves and made a final decision.   One other possibility for avoiding the draft was if a person could prove he was irreplaceable at his work or the business would collapse without him.   Not many men of draft age qualified for this exemption.   All these cases were also reviewed by the German authorities, and their swastika stamp was needed to be excused.

Some boys took very drastic actions to avoid the draft. An example is burning cut-up pieces of rayon stockings and collecting the ashes. These were mixed with water, and the boys drank this liquid. I never found out the medicine man for this recipe. The nylon stockings were brought into my country by German soldiers for their girl friends. Ashes from the synthetic material affected their liver, and in a couple of weeks' time, the young men looked ready to die. Their faces looked very grayish-pale, and they became so weak they could hardly walk. Their physical condition was accepted as not fit to serve in the German Army. Some of them proved to be not fit to live also, as they were not able to recover from the damaged liver and died. Being in the German Army was terrifying to our young men. The Germans called our newly drafted soldiers "volunteers," but we had only three choices: killing ourselves, going to a concentration camp, or serving in the German army. The only good news was that the first Latvian division formed would have a Latvian commander and officers.

Our soldiers had to wear German uniforms with a badge on the right arm close to the shoulder with the name "Latvia" and our national flag colors, red, white, red.

The military gear was provided by the Germans, and directions for military action were given by them. In April of 1942 I was seventeen, and I was hoping that in a year's time the war would be over. I was dreaming.

During the summer of 1942 I spent two months on the farm with relatives I had never met before. I was experienced farm help now, and they needed me.

I found out that in the area where the farm was, a number of other teenagers were spending the summer away from the city. Fresh air was one reason, but also we wanted bacon for our work. On Sundays we got together and played volleyball. One energetic boy from gymnasium said, "Maybe we city boys can come up with some form of entertainment that we can perform in the upcoming summer festival in the community center."

"Good idea," we agreed, "but what can we do?"

"Let's sing," somebody said.

Everybody agreed, and six of us started practicing; after the performance we became the "stars" of the evening.

My first stage experience had been almost disastrous. I was eight years old, and my dad decided that I had to play my violin at a police department Christmas party. I knew the number that I would be playing by heart, and could read music from the sheet that was placed in front of me on the stand. When I got on the stage by myself and saw all the people sitting quietly in the auditorium waiting for me to play, I froze. I couldn't remember my number nor could I see the notes on the sheet. After a few seconds I pulled myself together and I played. I knew my performance was not good, but I received applause anyway. Since then I've always understood when someone says they have stage fright. It's a terrible feeling.

This time being on the stage was different; I was older and I had the other boys for support.

When I returned home from the farm, more and more boys from my neighborhood and school were wearing uniforms. I didn't know about the Latvian Military Academy graduates, and how the draft was affecting them. They were older than twenty-five. I noticed many officers walking on the streets with Latvian national color badges. I assumed some of these were from our academy.

We had a few volunteers to the army. There were men whose lives, families, relatives or friends were ruined by the Communists, and they hated the Red Army so much they were anxious to fight them any chance they got.

After the war when I was in the Displaced Persons Camp in Germany, I met a man who was greatly decorated with medals for bravery. His name was Zanis Butka. He had been a farmer and family man with a wife and three daughters. An older lady, farm help, was living with them. A couple of months prior to the German occupation, he was working in the field close to the forest. He saw a strange car pull in near the farmhouse, and three men he didn't know stepped out and went inside the house. His fist started tightening, but he was afraid to go home. Soon they left, and after dark he went home. His wife told him that the KGB men were looking for him. The next morning he packed a few things and went to live in the forest. The forests in Latvia were much like a jungle, so thick it was almost impossible to walk through them. The forests saved many people's lives, as they provided a hiding place from the Communists and Germans.

Three days later a Russian military truck arrived, and he saw the Communists taking his wife and three young daughters away; that was the last time he saw his family. Would his family have been spared if he had come forward? No one knows, but probably not. In any case, his hatred of the Communists became a passion, and his need for revenge overwhelming. He knew that the older lady was still there and taking care of the animals. He stayed in the forest, because he was sure his farm was under surveillance. He returned to his home after the Germans occupied Latvia, but it was empty without his family. He had strong guilt for not coming forward to be taken instead of or with them.

He didn't have anything then to live for, and he wanted to kill all the Communists by himself. He volunteered for the German army. He was wounded five times for unbelievable feats in fighting the Red Army. There were times when he slept under Russian tanks and threw a hand grenade into the tank, blowing it up as he made his escape. A number of times he made entry into the Russian soldiers' bunker during the night, doing as much damage as possible with his gun and grenades. One night he was close to the Russian line in an observation position. The Russians knew he was nearby, and fired some shots into his suspected hiding place. He had to move to another location which was very wet. He lay down in a ditch, and being exhausted, he fell asleep. In the morning he found himself frozen in ice, but fortunately nothing had to be amputated.

The last time he was in the hospital he met a Latvian nurse. They got married soon after. He wanted to start a new family.

In the fall of 1942, a couple of weeks after school started, one morning I noticed a big sign on the bulletin board. It said that the farmers needed help to harvest their crops, such as red beets, cabbage and potatoes because their sons had been drafted into the service. I signed up, as did many other students. The help activities were planned for Saturday and Sunday. All schools in the city were involved. About a dozen students, including some gymnasium girls, were assigned to the same farm as I. The farmers treated us well; at the end of the second day there was not a potato left in the fields. It was an accomplishment and a different experience for most of the city kids.

I believe it was 1942 when I first saw the yellow star on the backs of some people being marched along the streets under armed guard. We were told that these people were being escorted to a factory to manufacture parts. I saw this at other times, and never understood why they were being guarded. I knew nothing of this, and didn't know until after the war what was happening to Jews. I do remember, though, the lady who lived downstairs talking to my mom one day and crying as she said that her employer, a Jewish tailor, and his family had given her their family silver to keep for them until they would return. They were supposedly being "re-located" to another place. At that time, she had a feeling that they were being sent to labor camps or something similar. She did not seem to have much faith that they would return. None of us had ever heard of the death camps. Our knowledge about everything was very sketchy and was totally controlled by the Germans.

One day at school I got a message from Konrads to see him after school; all the club members attended. He told us that Estonia had managed to establish a flight school for pilot training in the city, Bate, that was only ten kilometers from my city, Liepaja. He knew the questions we all had in our minds, but he didn't know if we would have a similar school or not. For me, approaching eighteen, and five others of draft age, this was interesting news. It gave us a new spark of hope to avoid the infantry. However, even if a flight school would be established at the same location as the Estonian school, what was our chance of getting in? There was no doubt in my mind, if I had a choice between the army (infantry) or the air force, which I would choose. The news was only five minutes old, and all agreed that we had to pursue it and get more information from the higher-ups. I was delegated to go to our capital city, Riga, and see Colonel Rucelis, who was in charge, about this new development. I was in Riga only once before at a Boy Scout jamboree.

Riga is the capital of Latvia, was founded in 1201 and is situated on the Daugava River, near the river's mouth on the Gulf of Riga, an arm of the Baltic Sea.

Riga consists of an old medieval city center, with narrow, winding streets and distinctive Gothic architecture, and new sections with a grid street plan and more modern buildings. An attractive sea coast of sand dunes to the west of the city is the site of a popular beach resort, the city of Jurmala.

Riga is a major sea port and manufacturing center. The port carries on an active commercial cargo trade with Western Europe and serves as the base for an Atlantic deep-sea fishing fleet.

As the cultural center of Latvia, the city is the seat of the Latvian University (1919) and of the Latvian Academy of Sciences.

I had an uncle living there who was a mailman. He offered help to find Colonel Rucelis, and he invited me to stay with his family as long as I wanted. I was wearing my new coat, boots, and my Technical School hat when I approached the tall building with high steps where the Colonel's office was located. I opened the heavy building entrance door and my curiosity about this man and my mission was growing. I didn't have an official appointment and I was rather nervous, but also determined. I knew if I had to come back ten times to get the information I needed, I would.

After I introduced myself to his secretary, a tall, slim man appeared, dressed in a Latvian Air Force uniform, black with silver trim. It had pilot wings on the left side plus some other decorations I didn't recognize. He stood at the door and kindly invited me into his office and introduced himself as Colonel Rucelis. I knew at once that he was the right man for me to talk with.

I explained why I was there and that I'd like to carry back as much information as possible to our club members. He looked at me very calmly and didn't seem to be pressed for time. We talked for about forty-five minutes. He saw the possibility of establishing a Latvian flight training school, but there were many negotiations and under-standings that needed to be resolved between the Germans and us. We didn't have any more our English-made

"Glosters" (fighting planes). They were destroyed after the Russian invasion. Finally, he said he couldn't promise, but the possibility of our having a flight school was good.

He gave me several application forms for our club members to be filled out and submitted to him for evaluation. I couldn't believe I was shaking hands with a colonel. At that time, he looked to me like God. I was, after all, a small town boy. I felt that there was some common electricity flowing between us during our conversation, and I was ecstatic at being able to talk freely to this important person and at having hopeful news to bring home.

1942 -- Riga, Latvia
With relatives and seeing Colonel Rucelis, finding out about
Latvian flight school.

Five of us filled out the forms, including Konrads. He was older than twenty-five and was not directly affected by the draft, but perhaps he would want to join the air force for the flying experience. The other older club members were undecided and took a "wait and see" position.

In January of 1943 I received a letter and order to report to the flight school in Bate. They had obviously established a Latvian school, and I was obviously accepted. After reading the letter, I started getting mixed feelings. I would have to leave my parents, brother, school, and my Aero Club friends. After thinking it over for several days I convinced myself that it was the right decision and that I was lucky to be accepted in the air force instead of being drafted into the infantry and fighting on the ground. In April I would be eighteen, anyway, and there was no chance I could have escaped the draft. My parents didn't want me to go anyplace if they had their way, but they didn't. In the final analysis, there was no choice.

9

In the beginning of December, 1942, the German army penetrated to the suburbs of Moscow. Battles were fought in the snow. The Germans were unprepared for winter warfare and suffered heavy losses. The Russians were showing that they still retained the power to attack, and they were winning battles. The German army was forced to take a defensive position.

One day early in December, my dad said, "Time to go to the forest and select a tree for Christmas."

We chose a tree about seven feet tall and placed it in the same place as in years before. We didn't have electric Christmas lights, but we used real twisted white candles with wax catchers. Family rules were strict; candles could be lit only at Christmas Eve when all the family was present. For decorations we used apples, specially made cookies and hand-made paper decorations of different colors. From day one when the tree was brought into the house, the pine aroma set me in a holiday mood. This Christmas we all wanted to be very close to each other, for soon after Christmas I would be eighteen and soon would be leaving home.

My brother was four years old, and I hope that he remembers this Christmas together. As it turned out, this was the last Christmas tree I ever lit in my Latvian home. On Christmas Day we all went to church.

After the holidays my dad wanted to have a family picture taken. That picture I carried with me during the war and after, always reminding me that once I had a family that I loved and who loved me.

Then February came and it was time for me to report for active duty. It was real; it wasn't like we used to play war games by the Baltic Sea. The day I was leaving, Dad gave me a piece of paper with hand-written paragraphs from the Bible.

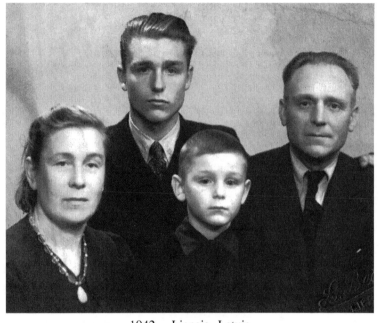

1942 -- Liepaja, Latvia
My family -- mother Anna, father Janis and brother Vilnis and myself.

The family picture and this piece of paper are the only things I have from my home, and I always have them with me. Big hugs and tears in my parents' eyes set me in a sad mood, but I had to go to catch the train. My parents and little brother rode with me on the streetcar to the train station. I think it was harder for them to see me go than it was for me. We all cried. My parents knew that it could be a long time -- and maybe never -- before I would come home again.

I walked across the street to the train station and boarded. I waved a last good-bye to my family out of the train window. They got smaller and smaller as the train pulled away from the station, and soon they disappeared from my sight. It was about ten miles to the newly established Luftwaffe base. I saw a large field surrounded by a high fence with a guarded entrance gate. I showed the guard my papers, and he opened the gate.

When I got inside the military installation everybody was wearing German Luftwaffe uniforms, gray color with yellow trim. Some distance away I could see planes. Then I noticed uniforms with Estonian colors, blue, black and white on the right arm. I couldn't speak to the Estonians because I didn't know their language. Two officers passed me with Latvian colors on their arms. I went to them and asked where I had to report. It was a good feeling; even if they wore Luftwaffe uniforms, they were my people. Soon I got used to seeing these uniforms. I was wearing one myself.

Once I knew where my bunk bed was located, all the rest was scheduled for me. All I had to do was just follow orders, and the most important thing was to be able to find my bed after an exhausting day of activities. Boys who didn't have any military training had to go through boot camp, and that included me.

In the Latvian facilities we had about fifty people. Some of them were trained earlier by German boot camp instructors. Some were officers from the Latvian Air Force, trained as flight instructors, and some of them were preparing for pilot qualification approval by the Germans.

Boot camp was tough, and I was glad I'd played a lot of soccer at home, so that I could run for a long time. It was scheduled for three months, seven days a week. If you were lucky you might get a couple of days' pass per month. Instructors were Germans and Latvians. No matter which, they were all a pain in the neck. They could ground you at any time, not give you a pass to leave the installation, or they could even stop you from getting into pilot training. Particularly, one German instructor who we called "Speece" gave us a very hard time. One night after midnight he walked into our sleeping quarters wearing black suede gloves. He touched the tops of the storage cabinets and found some dust. All we heard was a sudden loud yell, and in a few seconds we were all out in our underwear, barefoot, running and falling to the ground on command in the very cold snow for half an hour.

The first pass was granted after a month of training only if the instructor was satisfied with the progress that had been made. I got my pass for two days, and I was glad when I was able to go home. Before they let us go through the gate, we had to pass shoe, uniform, hair and nail inspection and demonstrate that we knew how to salute.

When I got home my parents were happy to see me, but not glad to see me wearing a German uniform. My mom said, "It looks strange." I turned my right arm and showed her my Latvian national colors and said, "Mom, this is who I am, just the same as I always have been." Sleeping in my own bed was wonderful. I managed to get several more passes to go home.

Konrads arrived about a week later and was hoping that he would be able to get into the flight school without going through boot camp. That was not possible. He was over twenty-five years old and he had the option to decide

1943 -- Bate, Latvia
In Flight School

whether he wanted to join the Luftwaffe or not. After finding out about boot camp, he decided that he would rather go back and finish building his own plane so that he could fly any time he wanted. We were all looking forward to having Konrads with us, and we were disappointed, but he had to make up his own mind.

During flight training we had a bad accident. Two of the students were performing solo (no instructor) turns. One was assigned to practice left turns, and the other was making right turns at different altitudes. One of them didn't pay close attention to the navigational instruments, and they crashed. Both were killed. One of them was a good friend of mine from the Aero Club. They received an honor guard funeral and reached the sky forever. It was a sad day.

At the end of September, training was completed and the first Latvian squadron was formed. Twelve two-seater planes, Arado-66, arrived from Germany and take-off was scheduled for the first week of October. The squadron consisted of twenty-two men. That included pilots, a Latvian-German interpreter, a physician, a chief mechanic and a bomb specialist. After the completion of flight school, I was the youngest, least experienced pilot flying motor propelled airplanes. Most of the time on our missions over Russia, I was assigned to the co-pilot's seat. During these missions I had about one hundred hours of air time.

Our planes were assigned as light bombers, carrying four bombs of approximately two hundred pounds each. Missions over Russia would be carried out during the night, and the daily mission instructions would be received from the Luftwaffe headquarters. The squadron commander was Latvian Captain Salmins.

Prior to our take-off, we were given four-day passes to go home and see our family, friends, sweethearts, and to cry a lot.

My home looked the same as when I left. It was winter, and I decided to try my skis to see if they still fit. They were fine, and I was skiing for awhile with the neighborhood kids who were still there. I went to visit Konrads and some other friends from my school. Konrads had made progress building his plane, and he was planning to have his first test flight in the spring. After visiting awhile I said to him, "Good luck Konrads," and we shook hands. It was the last time I ever saw him. This visit was also the last time I saw my brother.

When I returned to the base, a going away and accomplishment party was planned. It consisted of a glass of wine, cookies, and picture taking. That's all it was.

The next morning snow plows cleared the snow from the runway, and we were ready for takeoff. Two planes took off at the same time. We circled around our buildings several times, and everybody was out there waving to us. We didn't fly in formation, but two planes stayed close to each other. It was daylight, and we had some concern that we could be attacked by Russian MIG's.

Our destination was a small airport close to the Russian border and five kilometers from the city of Ludza. All planes landed safely and we noticed that somebody had made a "home" for us. It was an underground bunker with several entrances and twenty-two bunk beds with blankets. There was food in the "kitchen" area that consisted of a wood stove with a chimney leading outside the bunker. We chose our beds and placed our gear under them; we were pretty well situated. The bunker was about two hundred feet from the landing strip, leading to the forest behind and surrounded by smaller trees. There was at least a foot of snow on the ground. This bunker was not built for us, but I believe at some time Luftwaffe were previously using it. The underground bunker gave us protection and during the cold winter months, some warmth. You could walk two feet from the bunker and you wouldn't suspect that a bunch of humans were living there.

Some distance away from us was a small group that comprised a German engineering unit. They were responsible for running snow plows, preparing landing lights and providing communication systems. They also saw to medical supplies, stock bombs, mail delivery, cantina, and provided other assistance as needed.

Planes were stored during the day between trees, and were covered with white blankets for camouflage.

Food and cantina in the Luftwaffe were good. Cantina packages were delivered for each person once a month and contained all kinds of good things to eat, plus cigarettes. I didn't smoke, and sent all my cigarettes to my dad. I remembered that after the German occupation, cigarettes were not available at the store, and he was struggling with his smoking habit. He had started growing his own tobacco leaves in the back yard, drying them in the attic, and cutting and mixing them with cherry leaves.

Our kitchen stove in the bunker was also used for heating. We really had to watch out not to put too much wood in the stove. If we did, sparks started coming out of the chimney. We especially had to be careful during the night. We could see Russian planes pretty often, and we didn't want to send any invitations for company. Whenever fire was in the stove, one of us was watching the chimney.

At the beginning of December during the night we heard a big explosion. We ran outside, and some distance away we could see yellow smoke and flames against the dark sky. In the morning we found out that Russian guerrillas had blown up a German supply train close to the city of Ludza. We saw German Waffen S.S. all over the woods searching for the Russians. I felt a little safer, knowing that there were military units in the area besides us.

Soon Christmas was around the corner, and I started feeling sentimental. Remembering home, cutting and decorating the tree, and being with my family at the holidays occupied my thoughts. I was not the only one; everybody had similar feelings of wanting to be home during this season. Somebody asked what we were going to do to celebrate Christmas. Pipitis, our master mechanic, said, "We can make a snowman; that's about all." We wanted more than that, and we created a Christmas feeling by putting up a tree, and decorating it with whatever we could find.

One day, when Pipitis went to the woods to look for the right tree, he came home with a baby deer. He said, "Maybe the mother deer was shot by hunters, and the baby doesn't know what to do." We built a light fence around some trees, and Pipitis found a bottle and made something similar to a nipple that he could use to feed the baby deer. Milk was available. He didn't let anyone else feed the fawn. The little deer became our squadron talisman.

The cantina for December was very good, and we all put our goodies on the table. The Luftwaffe delivered four dozen bottles of red wine, and with that and our good food snacks and our tree, we celebrated Christmas the best we could. I was eighteen.

We were not allowed to leave our area without our commander's permission, and we didn't have anyplace to go, or any way to get there, anyway, so we tried to make our lives at least somewhat normal. We stayed at that location, flying night bombing missions over Russia till the snow started melting and the grass, under the snow blanket all winter long, was ready to start growing.

Our baby deer was about three months old, and she was feeling pretty comfortable with us, allowing us to touch her any time we wanted. When the time came that we were ordered to another location, Pipitis said, "Our little deer is old enough to survive and we have to let her go." He opened the fence and she started walking, then gracefully running into the forest. "Bye-bye, baby deer," Pipitis was shouting. The next day, as a surprise to everyone, she came back, and Pipitis insisted this was a sign that we should take her with us. Some simple modifications were needed to the plane to accommodate the fawn. None of us had had any previous experience with a deer; especially we didn't know how she would behave in the airplane.

At the new location we didn't have a bunker or barracks to live in. We had to negotiate with the nearby farmer to allow us to use his barn. Communication lines were opened with the Luftwaffe so that we could receive daily mission orders, cantina and mail that everybody looked forward to. The landing strip was walking distance from the barn.

Our baby deer, after the short ride, didn't show any discomfort, but maybe she was a little scared.

The farm was growing linen, and the fields surrounded the small building which housed the sauna. Close to the building was a large pond that was used for bleaching the linen fibers.

Inside the building in one corner was a large pile of rocks heated with wood. About four feet from the rocks were four wooden bleachers. Water was poured on the heated rocks to create steam. The steam was very hot and everybody started sitting on the first step till they got used to it and slowly progressed to the fourth step. Each person carried a specially made small wooden bucket with water to cool off the face and head and a bundle of birch tree twines with dried-out leaves. Once a person started getting comfortable sitting on the fourth step he started striking his body with birch twines; the feeling was like touching the body with hot wire. The person then ran outside and jumped into the cold water pond and returned to the fourth step to sit for awhile. Next a bucket of cold water was poured over the body to seal the pores. This method of bathing was used for centuries by our people. It was very invigorating. We asked our medical doctor if this method was still good. He said, "It is the best way of bathing," but he cautioned us not to stay for too long in the cold pond.

The farmer allowed us to use his sauna any time we wanted with the exception of Friday nights. This was family night, and everybody in the family went at the same time without being embarrassed about their naked bodies. I liked the sauna. I used to go with my dad to the city sauna, built for public use. Our city sauna had wet steam coming out of the boiler and was not as good as steam from heated rocks.

The planes were hidden in the woods and covered with camouflage to prevent visibility from the sky. So far we hadn't had any conflict with Russian MIG's patrolling the sky in the morning. The Russian MIG-12 was the best fighter plane they had at that time. Their capability was

1944 -- Latvia, close to Russian border. Latvian first squadron pilots prior to the mission.

close to German ME-9 fighter planes. One morning two MIG-12's attacked us. We didn't have any anti-aircraft guns around that area for protection. We had foxholes which we jumped into and hoped for the best. It is always terrifying to have someone shooting at you. After this attack we learned that the MIG's were modified, having a gun installed in the tail, where previously there was not one. They were shooting coming and going.

The sun started getting warmer as summer arrived. I liked this time of year, seeing new leaves on the trees, flowers blooming and green grass everywhere.

We received orders to relocate inside Russia in the vicinity of the city Vekikiye-Luki. When we received this move, Pipitis said, "Now we have to leave our baby deer in Latvia's woods so she can find deer friends and have a family." It was sad to see her go; we all loved her.

The new airfield was pretty sizable, and six ME-9's were ready for action. The Latvian 19th division was fighting the Russians around that area, and we were sent to help them. Also we would have shorter distances to fly on our bombing missions. During the night we were trying to destroy Russian tanks moving on the road and ammunition depots in the woods. We were dropping bombs on their military installations, never letting them have a good night's sleep.

The airfield was surrounded by swamplands, and I have never, before or since, seen so many mosquitos in my life. We had the all-body mosquito net and spray, but that didn't stop them from attacking us by the million, or so it seemed. Somehow they managed to find openings in the net and go after our blood. I almost couldn't see the sun, as it was covered with mosquitos like a black cloud. Their buzzing noise was worse than artillery shelling. Fortunately, we didn't stay long at that location and moved to another place in Russia.

Seven of our pilots were officers, Latvian Air Force Academy graduates who were flying Glosters during our independence days. I particularly admired one of our pilots. His name was Janic Muiznicks. He was not an officer, but was flying planes with the Aisargi organization before the war. I had noticed his intelligence sometime before; he was very particular with everything, including his blanket. He marked one end of the blanket so that he wouldn't place his feet end of the blanket to his face. He was our "cheerleader," and in the evenings prior to the missions while waiting for the Luftwaffe's orders, he liked to play the accordion and always attracted a crowd who liked to sing along. Later on, I found out that he was a professor at the University of Riga, teaching aerodynamics. He came up with the idea that penetrating the wood with high pressure forcing a certain liquid into the grain would considerably increase the strength of the wood. This would allow less wood to be used for plane construction. thereby reducing weight. He demonstrated feasibility, and the British were interested in his development; they accepted the concept and re-designed several of their military planes, including Glosters.

Prior to World War II, wood was used as construction material for many planes. In later years aluminum, magnesium, and titanium started replacing wood for strength and weight reasons.

The Latvian second squadron, flying similar planes to ours, were mission ready in May, but we never stayed at the same location. From school in Bate, a number of trained pilots were chosen and sent to Germany for F-190 special training. The F-190 was a fighter plane with the capability to carry bombs for low-altitude execution. Many German pilots preferred F-190's to ME-9's. After training in January, F-190 squadrons were formed and, as a surprise to our pilots, they were ordered to attack American and British bombers flying out of England to Germany. When our men saw British bombers coming, they all bailed out into the Atlantic Ocean without firing a round. They were all picked out of the ocean by the British Navy, and were put in a British prisoner of war camp. After the British understood the position of the Latvians, who had been forced into the German military, the prisoners were treated well. If the Germans had rescued our men at sea, our men would surely have been shot as traitors or for not following orders. The initial agreement we had with the Germans was that our military would be involved only on the eastern front fighting Russians. That agreement included our pilots.

Germany was weakening as a military power, and Russian armies were stronger and better equipped than they had ever been. They started winning more and more battles, taking their territory back from the Germans. They were getting closer to our borders.

We got orders to leave Russia, and we landed in an airport in the eastern part of Latvia; close to the main highway entering Russia. After several weeks at that location, we could see German military vehicles moving in both directions, east and west, on the highway.

One day was different. We noticed massive German forces pulling out of Russia, and they were moving west towards Germany on the highway. Not a single vehicle was moving east. There was a continuous flow of military gear all day and night. There were still some battles fought some distance away, and we could hear artillery shelling. Pipitis said, "The Russians are coming back." Our hearts sank.

The next day was a beautiful fall morning. The sun was bright and we were surrounded by tall birch trees; their leaves had started yellowing. That morning the military vehicles were still moving on the highway, and we had a strong feeling that we would be flying out soon.

The day before, one of our planes had developed engine problems. We didn't want to leave the plane if we could help it. Our master mechanic, Pipitis, concluded that a bad valve was causing the problem. He removed the eight cylinder straight block engine head and disassembled the valve from the head. The valve was bad, but he thought that he might be able to fix it. He needed valve lapping compound, but he didn't have it. He asked us if we could find a piece of clear glass and a couple of stones. Pipitis started pounding the piece of glass with the stone to make a fine powder. He mixed it with oil and started lapping. After twenty minutes the valve looked pretty good. It was close to noon time, and there was no traffic on the highway anymore. Artillery shelling and machine gun noises were gone, and it was very quiet. I didn't like that, and I remembered my dad saying, "There is no wind before a storm." All other planes were ready for takeoff, but we wanted to wait and hope that Pipitis would be able to save the plane. I got binoculars and climbed into a tree to look east as far as I could to see if the Russians were coming.

The valve installation was completed and the head installed; it was ready to test. The engine started, but we had to see if it had enough power to pull the plane off the ground. The engine didn't develop full thrust but enough to fly. We were so relieved that the plane was saved. Salmins had given the order that we would fly next to our capital city, Riga. Thanks to the miracle performed by Pipitis, we would all be flying there together.

Later on we heard more about the situation in the eastern Latvia location we left at that time. About an hour after we left, Russian troops were marching on that ground. We got out just in time. Closer to Riga, the Germans had a tank division and power to strike, but the Russians were moving from the Lithuania side toward Riga. That night we did very heavy bombing on the road in Lithuania where hundreds of tanks and other Russian military vehicles were moving on the road during the night. We began to realize we were seriously short of fuel, as we couldn't fill up after our last mission. We knew that the days were numbered before Latvia would be taken over again by the Communists. This was a terrible prospect but it was true. Before Christmas, 1944, most of the country was taken, with the exception of the Curland Pocket, close to the Baltic Sea, where the Latvian 15th Division fought it out with the Russians. Hitler shot himself April 30, 1945, but Latvian soldiers fought until May 15 waiting for help from England that never came.

However, this was still late 1944, and we took off from Riga the next morning and landed at Bate, the airstrip so familiar to us. This was where we had received our training and had taken off as a squadron. Here was our home base, but nobody was here. The airplanes were gone, no uniformed men could be seen, and the buildings were empty. Only the high fence with the gate that I had first walked through one year and nine months ago was still there. We found two guards, who told us that two weeks earlier school was evacuated and relocated to Denmark after the Russians increased bombing over Liepaja and some other places along the Baltic Sea. We didn't have communication with anybody, including the Luftwaffe. All decisions were made by our squadron commander, Salmins. That's the way we wanted it. Nobody knew where we were.

My hometown, Liepaja, was ten kilometers (six miles) from the base. Four of us asked Salmins if we could have a pass to the city. I hadn't seen my family for a whole year, and I wanted to see them badly.

He said, "Be back at seven o'clock in the morning. The decision will be made by then as to what we will be doing from now on."

I left the base in the late afternoon and walked and ran, and by the time I got home, it started getting dark. I was so excited at the prospect of seeing my parents and my brother, I ran upstairs. The light on the entrance door was not lit. I knocked at the door, but nobody answered. I was alarmed.

For some time I hadn't received mail, or it had been received very late; I wasn't the best letter writer, either. I hadn't had any communication with home for several months. We had moved around a lot, and didn't know what had happened to our mail. When they didn't answer the door, I was filled with dread. What could have happened to them?

I ran downstairs to see the lady who had made my coat. She opened the door, and was surprised to see me. She said my mom was always worried about me and would be so happy to see that I was all right. Then the roof caved in for me when she said my brother was in the hospital. Four days before, the city was heavily bombed by the Russians. My five-year-old brother was playing in the front yard, and was hit on the right elbow by shrapnel. The injury was severe. I wanted to see him, but didn't have enough time to go to the hospital and also see my parents. They had temporarily moved out of the city to live in the country with relatives. I knew the farm was about twenty kilometers (twelve miles) from home in the same direction as the base where I had to be back at seven o'clock in the morning.

The neighbor lady sounded so sad, I believed she had great concern about what would happen to my family. She gave me a hug, and I started running. Twenty kilometers was a long way to go, but I got a ride with a horse and wagon part of the way, and it wasn't too bad. By the time I got to the farm it was two o'clock after midnight. My parents were up and couldn't believe that I was actually with them, alive and well. I had only two hours time. It was a sad and difficult conversation. I could see the sadness in my mom's and dad's faces when they talked about my brother and the suffering he was enduring. There was the possibility of his even losing the arm. In addition, they were very concerned about me, and about the prospects for our country. My parents understood the situation, that Communists would soon be knocking on the door again. They were helpless to try to escape by leaving the country as many people were doing, especially with my brother in the hospital. My dad said, "We cannot take Vilnis out of the hospital and go on the road with no medical attention, not knowing where the next bed and food will be; he will never survive." He said they would stay at the farm or back home until my brother was well, and if it was possible then to leave the country, they would try. As it turned out, there was not enough time; my home and relatives' farm were taken by the Red Army after two weeks.

Dad said, "Many people are trying to find a way to leave the country on ships or boats to Sweden or the west. Some have even started walking west, hoping that they will be far enough away that the Red Army won't catch them." No one had any desire to live under the Communists again.

My parents agreed that I had three options: to stay in my country and be taken by the Russians as a prisoner of war, and probably be sent to a forced labor camp, to find a hiding place in the forest and try to live there until the Communist system might change in a few years, which was not likely, or to leave my country and try to find someplace else in the world to start a new life. Dad encouraged me to leave the country saying, "You are strong enough to take hard times and survive. The future for you here would be very dark."

I felt very bad to leave my parents and brother. My parents had given me a good life and childhood. I loved them. Now when they were getting older and needed me, I would not be there. But if I stayed there I could not help them anyway, and would no doubt create a danger to them. I felt like I was standing on quicksand and could be sucked in at any time. The war was not over and there was danger ahead of me and for them no matter what I did.

Dad said, "Our lives are in God's hands, and we don't know what will be next." He said a prayer for me, and they gave me one last hug. It was time for me to start running back to the base, and to let the wind dry my tears. It was the last time in my life that I saw my parents.

Soon after I got back, Salmins said, "We will fly to Liepaja's airport." This was the same place where I was flying gliders and went skiing on the snow covered hills during winter.

Flying time was short and we landed around ten o'clock in the morning. Salmins gave us our options, and they were about the same as my dad had said; we were free to make our own decision. Everybody wanted to leave the country. Staying in Latvia was sure death or imprisonment.

We had German planes but a Latvian commander; that made decision making easier as he was one of us. Our first choice was Sweden, a neutral country and friendly to Latvia. Salmins asked us to check how much fuel we had in the tanks. Head winds were strong that morning, and we had to cross the Baltic Sea. There was not enough fuel for all the planes to make it to Sweden. Our next choice was Danzig, a sizeable city on the Baltic Sea that belonged to Poland and had been taken over by the Germans. We all had enough fuel for this trip.

On October 11, 1944, at one o'clock in the afternoon we started our engines to be ready to leave our country. At low altitude south of us we could see artillery tracer bullets going in both directions; another tank battle was being fought. Salmins wanted us to fly far in and low over the Baltic Sea to avoid conflict with Russian submarines in the sea. Before we started our trip to Danzig we circled several times around Liepaja, and for the last time I saw silhouettes of my home, neighborhood, and the Baltic Sea shoreline. Home and my country looked to beautiful. Would I ever see them again?

10

We landed in the Danzig airport. The interpreter, who spoke five languages, including fluent German, went to the Luftwaffe's building to clear with the authorities our food supplies and cantina for our next destination close to the city of Hochensalz.

Hochensalz was a small city about forty kilometers north of Pozen. The city was surrounded by farm lands and had belonged to Poland, but was taken over by the Germans. It was a nice and quiet place to be. There were no signs that war had ever been in this area.

Salmins said, "From now on we have to report every morning at seven o'clock until further notice. The rest of the day you can do whatever you want." The war was not over and we couldn't believe what we heard. We thought it would be only for a few days, but we stayed for four weeks. This place was like living in heaven. The war zone was far enough away that we couldn't hear any shooting and didn't have any air raids. There were cities nearby which were bombed by the Americans and British. Apparently there was nothing to bomb in Hochensalz.

Finally we had to give up our heaven and our airplanes. Fuel was not available for us to fly to Denmark, where we wanted to go. The city of Varde in Denmark was our new destination, but we had to go by train. For the last time we touched our planes and started walking to the city to catch the train.

In Varde we joined our Latvian ex-school comrades, who were also wearing Luftwaffe uniforms. Colonel Rucelis was in charge of this operation of about one hundred fifty people. He was the man I had met in Riga wearing the Latvian black uniform almost two years ago. We really didn't know our purpose for being there, but getting further away from the war zone was a good enough reason for us.

One day I met a man from the Aero Club and asked how Konrads was doing. He told me that during the summer Konrads was flying his own plane that he had built and was very proud of it. In September when the Russians started coming back, he flew to Sweden in his two-seater plane and took his mother out of Latvia and returned for his father. All the family were now situated in Sweden.

I was not surprised to hear that Konrads had accomplished the "mission impossible" in getting his parents out of Latvia. I was sad, though, realizing the price they all had to pay. His parents, like all who fled, had to leave behind all their possessions, including their home and the wood-working shop. They had only the clothes they wore, and perhaps a very few of their most cherished possessions. I did not believe that my parents and brother had managed to escape. I dreaded thinking how their lives would be in Communist-controlled Latvia.

There were many German soldiers in Varde, but the Danes in the city were not friendly with them. The Germans never walked alone on the streets, but always were two or more together. They couldn't go to the stores either. The Danes wouldn't sell anything to them, keeping their products under the table when they saw German soldiers coming. At first the same treatment applied to us. We were not Germans, but were wearing the uniforms. Soon, the Danes understood our position, and after that we could go any place we wanted and buy whatever we desired.

My favorite place was a dairy products store. Nothing was rationed and we could buy anything that was available.

We pointed at what we wanted and showed how much. The Danish language was totally new to us, but we found ways for mutual understanding. It was an unusual sight seeing that much food in the stores. While living for a month in German-occupied Poland, we couldn't even find a potato to buy.

I was noticing several unusual things in that city. In the morning women were on their knees scrubbing the concrete path from the house to the sidewalk on the streets. Seeing packages lying by the mailboxes on the sidewalks for the postman was not unusual. Apparently the people were very honest.

I noticed some girls wearing scarves and looking like old ladies, but I was told that the girls were being punished by Danish boys for seeing German soldiers. Through their hair a channel was cut right in the middle. It looked very funny, and must have been humiliating for the girls. They covered it up with scarves.

Speaking of girls, we managed to meet a few ourselves. It's true we didn't know each other's language, but we didn't seem to have much trouble communicating. In fact, I had a girl friend all the weeks we were in Denmark. She didn't speak Latvian and I didn't know any Danish. We managed.

We were living in a barracks. One afternoon a German SS unit moved in and ordered everybody to move out on the street immediately. They lined us up and ordered us to march out of the city, with several SS men following. I felt like I was in a prison camp. We couldn't understand what this was all about. After a couple of hours we could return and found out that our barracks had been raided. We heard that the night before, military weapons had been parachuted close to our area by English bombers. The Germans were suspicious that we might be collaborating with the Danish underground. The next day our officers received orders to prepare for moving closer to the North Sea and to dig in for attack. Who would be attacking us? We were far away from the Russians. The Germans looked very nervous, and we speculated about what was happening. Perhaps they were afraid that the British were planning to land troops on the Danish coast and they wanted us to guard sections of it. That was not acceptable to our officers; we were not infantrymen, and never would fight British or Americans. The situation was similar to that of our F-190 pilots who abandoned many airplanes in the Atlantic Ocean after being ordered to attack British and American bombers. I have never understood just what authority the Germans had in Denmark at that time. They obviously had some kind of control over us, at least, but it was not absolute. They did not behave as occupiers, and the Danes did not treat them as such; they in turn did not trust the Danes nor us.

The next day we were split up into smaller groups and started heading for the train to move on to different locations. I was in a group of about fifty, and our assigned destination was Königsberg, close to Lithuania and to the war zone.

When I got on the train I started feeling very weak and went to see the doctor who was with us. He looked in my eyes and said that I had jaundice, and I would have to go to the hospital as soon as we arrived in Königsberg. He said, "You can get jaundice from eating rich food that your liver can't handle." I had plenty of whipping cream and other goodies almost every day from the Danish store. After being on a lean diet for a long time, it tasted so good. He assigned me to the Luftwaffe hospital, and when I arrived there, the sparkling cleanliness struck my eyes.

I was told that all regular beds were taken, and my bed would be placed in a hallway. It was fine with me, and in some ways even better than I expected. I didn't have to see and listen to wounded people suffering and in pain. I never saw so many wounded and sick people before.

I was on the third floor. One day the nurse told me that on the first floor were two more Latvians. The first week I was not allowed to leave my bed, but later I could walk on my floor only. I wanted to visit the Latvians on the first floor, so at the first opportunity I sneaked down. They both had severe injuries, but were glad to see somebody who spoke the same language.

Christmas, 1944 was only a few days away, and the hospital distributed small gifts. They said that on Christmas Eve there would be hot red wine with cloves available to the patients who could drink. I didn't ask my doctor if I could have wine or not, but it was Christmas Eve, and I went to the place where it was being distributed. I got three glasses and went to the first floor to visit my new Latvian friends, and to take them Christmas wine. We all agreed that we could think of better places than a hospital to celebrate Christmas, and we drank to that. After awhile, I went back to my floor and fell asleep. Suddenly I woke up and felt like my bed was spinning; soon all the red wine I had drunk was on my white sheets. I looked around to see if anybody had witnessed what happened. It was pretty late, and only night lights were on. Nobody was visible. I wanted very much to cover up my indiscretion, so no one would witness my embarrassment. I knew the closet where the nurses kept clean bed sheets and laundry bags. After awhile I started feeling a little better, and I took the wine-covered sheets off my bed, put them in a laundry bag, and took clean ones from the closet. I changed my sheets, and in the morning when the nurse came to take my temperature, I looked like an angel sleeping in white sheets.

Soon after Christmas, the doctor told me that I would be released, and I would be receiving a month of health recovery leave. He wanted to know where I would like to go so that he could complete my release papers. One of the nurses offered me the opportunity to stay on her parents' farm, but I chose Pozen in Poland. I was not willing to chance an involvement with a German family. When we had been living in Hochensalz where we had left our planes, I heard about the city of Pozen. I didn't know anybody in Germany or Poland, so this town was as good as any. I received a hand full of papers and money, polished my shoes and started looking for the train that would take me to Pozen.

Pozen was a large, historical city and in some areas the architecture, parks, streets and streetcars reminded me of Riga. I took walks on the streets and liked to ride the streetcars. I stayed in some kind of hotel.

Walking on the street I noticed two soldiers wearing green uniforms with Latvian colors on the arm. We met several times; it was so good to be able to speak easily the language I knew. They showed me around. They were in the city for the same reason I was.

One morning we were waiting for the streetcar, and two good-looking girls stood in front of us. One of us said in Latvian, "Look, such nice legs."

The girl turned around and said in Latvian, "They are my legs and don't belong to you."

We started blushing and were so shocked that we forgot to start a conversation. We hadn't thought that there might be girls in town who spoke Latvian. Possibly, they were from German families who moved out from Latvia and settled in Pozen prior to the Russian occupation, or maybe they were real Latvian girls. Whoever they were, they were gone before we woke up and got to know them.

After about two weeks, the news said that Russians were in the city of Lodz, close to Pozen. I didn't like this news; I still had two weeks leave to spend in the city and look for adventures, but it was time for me to leave.

We decided to leave in the morning and to meet at the railroad station. I planned to go back to Königsberg, and my travel orders were issued from that city. I had them in my hands to buy a train ticket, but as soon as I opened the railroad station door I noticed a German military policeman inside, and soldiers lined up by the wall. Gray uniforms were at the right side, green at the left. I started walking through the entrance room and was stopped. I showed my papers to the army officer. He said I needed more travel approval stamps and pointed to the right wall. My new friends were sent to the left. Now what? It was a wait and see situation, and I was trapped. There was nothing I could do.

About eighty of us in gray uniforms were herded into a room for a couple of hours. Then the military police said that we had to go to another building. They lined us up in four rows and we started marching. We marched through the city streets and kept walking on a country road with farm houses on both sides. In the distance were larger buildings by the sides of the road. Armed military police with machine guns were at the front and back of the lines. I sensed the situation, and as far as another approval for travel, that was just plain baloney. The war zone was close and the Russians were gaining ground. The Germans needed all the help they could find. They had caught me like a fish in a net, and that was the reason I was marching; we were headed for the front lines. I didn't like the situation at all. I was sure I was on my way to becoming cannon fodder. I was trying to figure out what I could possibly do.

Soon I noticed on the road a farmer coming from the opposite direction with a horse and hay wagon. I was walking on the far left row; suddenly a thought came to me.

What would be the possibility to get on the other side of the hay wagon, and what would be the consequence if I got caught? I rapidly thought it through. My life was very tenuous anyway; what did I have to lose? I had only a few seconds to make up my mind. Did I have the nerve? My decision was made only as the opportunity was next to me. It was now or never. Part of me prayed that none of the other marchers would give me away. I was also praying that the armed guard only a few soldiers behind and to the right of me would not see me fall out of line. I was afraid my pounding heart would give me away. When the hay wagon got just opposite me I made a very swift turn to the left behind the wagon, and stayed behind a wheel so the military police wouldn't see my feet. It was obvious that several of the marchers saw me bail out, but nobody said anything. I was waiting for the guard to call out to me. My heart stopped for a few minutes till I knew I had made it. When the last military policeman with a machine gun was past the hay wagon, I breathed a deep sigh of relief. The farmer never knew I had taken refuge beside his wagon. I felt very lucky to still be alive and not to be heading for the war.

It was light outside and I had to find a place to hide until it got dark. A little way from the road I noticed a ditch with foliage, and I jumped in. It was several hours until dark and I had time to reflect on what had happened, and to think about what I could have done if I had been marching on the right hand side instead of the left. I would have had no chance to escape, and would by now be securely trapped. I thanked God for helping me stay alive. I felt more or less free again.

After dark I walked back to the railroad station and very cautiously approached, but didn't go through it. I went straight to the train. The destination for each train was posted, and I found one going to Königsberg. I didn't have a ticket, but didn't see that as a problem; I still had money.

On the train I felt fairly safe having papers and travel orders to return to my unit in Königsberg. I didn't know whether my group was still there. When the train stopped, they announced that this the last train from Pozen entering into this area. I realized that once again, luck was with me. I was on the last train into the heart of Germany from Pozen. The Communists were surrounding me, and who knows what would have been ahead if I hadn't caught this train? When I got to the barracks, my unit was still there.

A few days after my arrival, in the late afternoon, military ambulances started coming in, one after another with wounded German soldiers from the front lines. At least two hundred were brought in. One doctor and two nurses were all the help that was available. We gave up our beds and helped the medical people as much as we could. I had never had such an experience. There were men with all kinds of wounds everywhere, and more coming all the time. It was the first time I had seen people with arms dangling and every other kind of wound imaginable. They were crying and screaming in pain. I felt so sorry for all of them, Germans or not. I would not have made a good medic or doctor.

In the morning the Germans lined us up. We were about fifty Latvians. They gave us our orders, splitting us up into smaller groups to be assigned to different German units away from this location. They called our names and gave each of us a piece of paper with name, unit assigned, location and person to report to. Two German military vehicles were waiting for us and after three or four hours drive, we were distributed to different locations to German units. At one stop they called my name and Janis Kalnins.

I could see a high fence surrounding a large area with big guns inside. We walked through the guarded gate and reported to the person whose name was on the paper. We received a short orientation, and he showed us the barracks and beds where we would be staying. The Germans were wearing gray uniforms with red trim, but Janis and I had yellow trim. I knew that red means artillery duties, and it was obvious that personnel at that location were operating eight big guns (80 millimeter), the biggest the Germans had. All I knew about these guns was seeing them in pictures, and Janis acknowledged that he didn't know any more than I. We learned that we were about a hundred fifty miles south of Königsberg and not very far from the city of Lodz, the same city that was taken by the Russians when I was in Pozen.

Guns were set on a concrete pad about six feet deep in the ground and about twenty feet around. In the bunker walls, rectangular storage compartments were built for each individual shell, which were marked red and black. Red were for anti-aircraft and black for anti-tank firing. At least several hundred were stored in the bunker. The big guns were separated at least a hundred feet apart. Smaller guns for fast moving and low altitude aircraft were located around the big guns. Each big gun bunker had several trenches built for personal protection. At this location the guns had a very powerful firing capacity. I never learned what they were protecting.

We didn't have any assigned duty there, and it looked like nobody was busy, but they were prepared for fast action.

I had never met Janis before; one of the Germans was calling him Johan, the German interpretation of his name. One day I laughingly said to him, "You are wearing a German uniform, eating their food, and following their orders; I think I have to call you Johan." He laughed and said maybe that would be simpler while the Germans had us. Later Johan told me that he was a bronze medal winner in 1940 in the Oslo, Finland Olympics as a fast-walker. I noticed before that I had to take two or more steps for one of his. He was taller and older than I. He was a very nice person, quiet and pleasant.

One morning when we were ready to go to the mess hall for breakfast, the installation alarm went off. That meant that in seconds we had to be in our bunkers. A few minutes later ten Russian MIG-12's started buzzing over our heads and attacked the big gun base. I ran into the trench as fast as I could. MIG's were flying too fast and too low for the big guns to be used. Only smaller guns were firing rounds, trying to hit the MIG's. After the first attack, the MIG's returned several times. It lasted about fifteen minutes but seemed much longer. I though that attack would never end. After the MIG's finally left, I walked closer to the big gun and found two Germans shot dead and lying on the ground. I looked for Johan and couldn't find him at first. He was all right but slow getting out of the trench.

Some distance away two big guns were blown up. Possibly the guns surrounding the shells were hit and exploded. Damage was seen all over the place. The kitchen was ripped apart, some barracks were damaged, ten Germans were killed and more wounded.

I said to Johan, "What are we doing here? It doesn't make sense even to stay one more day. We are not German soldiers." My assessment of the situation was that Russian planes would return soon and would try to knock out all the big guns and then move in with their tanks and infantry. We didn't want to be with the Germans, but being caught by the Russians was even worse.

Johan agreed that we had to get out of there. We were surrounded by the high fence, and the guards were still at the gate. We were worried about trying to escape, but were determined to do it. We decided to dress like guards if we could, and to try to bluff our way out.

It was January and some snow was on the ground. We didn't have heavy winter coats like the guards were wearing. We went to the supply barracks and chose some coats and other heavy clothing we were missing, plus hand grenades and ammunition for the P-38 pistol and the rifles we had. We just acted like we belonged there, and no one questioned us. After dark we put our gear on and put into our pockets some bread we had picked up from the kitchen. We walked to the gate and tried, in our very limited German, to explain to the German guard that we had assigned duty to patrol the road outside along the fence. He believed us and opened the gate. We were free -- or at least outside the fence of the base.

We were walking north, and wanted to get as far as we could, not knowing what they would do when they noticed our absence. During the night we started hearing a shooting noise and it made us very uneasy. After we had walked about five miles, suddenly as from nowhere, two soldiers in white camouflage with machine guns jumped out from the bushes and yelled at us, "Stop!" We identified ourselves and said that our unit was broken up and we were heading to Königsberg. I asked if we were going in the right direction. He said, "This road will take you right to the city." We walked on, and they let us go.

Another mile and another surprise. We started hearing tank rattling noises coming from the right side of the field. We didn't have any way of knowing if the tanks were German or Russian. It wouldn't make much difference; we were in serious trouble either way. We hid behind some trees and tried to see if we could spot something moving. The night was just too dark, and after awhile the noise stopped, and we walked till daybreak. We were tired and started looking for a place we could stretch our legs and sleep.

There was a farm some distance away from the road, and it looked like nobody lived there. We sneaked into the shed where firewood was stored. We lay down and fell asleep. Our rifles we put on the wood pile and left; they were too heavy to carry. We still had our P-38.

In the morning we tried to reason out some strategy as to where we were going, but there were too many unpredictables and variables. We decided we had to just live day by day. Heading to Königsberg close to the Baltic Sea was the best we could figure out. We had about one hundred thirty miles to walk and no food.

We noticed military vehicles moving in both directions, and it looked like some farmers with horses and wagons full of their belongings were heading north too.

We didn't want to ask the military nor the farmers for a ride. We tried to minimize exposing ourselves as much as we could to German military and civilians. Our main problems were that we were young and healthy and didn't speak German. We could be mistaken for spies dropped by the British or Americans. At that time, the Germans were very wary, because they had discovered British and American soldiers wearing German uniforms walking on their land. The enemy were blowing up bridges and committing other acts of sabotage. Most days we felt safer walking through fields and generally keeping a low profile.

For more than two weeks we were without food, and we started getting desperate. We were not, as we had hoped, to Königsberg. Getting there was proving to be very slow, as we were walking a little and hiding a lot in the fields and forests.

We saw a farm up a hill, and said to each other, "Let's go there and find out if we can do some work for food." The farmer said he could use some help and showed us big water containers used for household needs and for animals. The containers were empty, and he gave us each two buckets and a flat piece of wood bar that was especially made for carrying water buckets over the shoulders. The water well was down the hill, and it took us at least two hours to fill the containers. The farmer gave us four slices of dark rye bread each, and we were ready to leave. Suddenly a uniformed SS man came out from the other door into the kitchen and wanted to take us to the town. We tried to explain that our unit was waiting for us to return, and we had to be there. He didn't accept our explanation, and for the next few seconds the tension was thick in the room. We were very scared. It was a question of who would draw his pistol first. I was not sure if someone was behind the door, maybe more SS men. We turned around and started walking to the door, hoping that he wouldn't shoot us in the back; he didn't, and we kept walking. The farmer had apparently reported us. Königsberg was still a good day's walking distance.

We found a newspaper saying that west of Königsberg the Red Army had reached a waterway at the Baltic Sea. I carried a map of Germany with me, and by looking at it, we got a better understanding of the situation. The Russians had broken through the German line and were occupying a narrow zone between Königsberg and Danzig. The waterway was inland from the Baltic Sea, and a strip of land connected the two cities. The Russians were not at the Baltic Sea yet. Including the water, we were surrounded by them. To get on the west side of the Russians, we had to find a ship from Königsberg-Pillow that would take us further west or find a way to cross at least a mile of water narrows by the city of Pillow. If we could cross the water we would be on a sandy beach stretching to the city of Danzig.

South of Königsberg we noticed heavy German tanks and other military concentration in a suburb of the city.

We though that maybe they were getting ready to break the Russian line.

We were stopped at road blocks twice by military police, but looking straight in their eyes and lying about our destination, we managed to get through the city and found a smaller road going to Pillow about twenty miles from Königsberg. I realized I was becoming a good liar, but there was no choice; survival was our first priority. There were many ambulances and vehicles with wounded soldiers going to Pillow. Maybe a ship was waiting for them? But what chance would we have of getting on such a ship, we asked ourselves. The answer, we knew, was none. If we shot ourselves in the leg or arm, then maybe. We weren't ready to do that, so we kept walking. Soon it was time to look for a bed, and we found one, next to the road in a hay barn. We were so hungry; it was again more than two weeks since we had had more than a little bread to eat. The best thing was to fall asleep, so we wouldn't have to think about it.

Early in the morning I heard voices on the road. I opened the barn door and peeked out. The road was full of civilians carrying handbags. Most of them were women and children. Suddenly I recognized spoken Latvian words. It was like beautiful music. I couldn't believe what I was hearing and ran outside. Johan was right behind me. It was just a miracle that we had found two Latvian families in a crowd of several hundred people. That they were speaking just at the time they passed the barn, and that I just happened at that moment to be peeping through the barn door, compounded the miracle.

They each carried a bag of their belongings and they offered us some clothing. They said, "It might be better if you looked like civilians." Most of the refugees were Germans who had been told that there would be a ship in Pillow to take them further west. We accepted our countrymen's clothing offer with thanks. We too felt that we would be better off in civilian clothes as refugees than in German uniforms looking like deserters. The most important thing for us, though, was to have some kind of document with the German eagle stamp. I got a food ration book from Latvia; they didn't need that any more. I became Karlis Zarins, about ten years older than my actual age. That was no problem, as people always told me I looked older. Johan got some kind of work book with a German eagle stamp, and he became Janis Klavins. Both families were from Liepaja, but didn't know my parents. I was thinking that they had so little for themselves in the bags they were carrying, and yet they were willing to share with us. Maybe they had even saved our lives. There were still generous people in the world.

I kept my "soldier book" (military I.D.) in my socks and didn't want to throw it away. That was the only document I had with my real name on it.

We went back to the barn and changed, but put our uniforms in the corner and covered them up with hay so we could find them if we changed our minds. We joined a refugee crowd and walked straight to the barracks in the city. The barracks rooms were full, so we slept in a hallway. As soon as we familiarized ourselves with the place, we went to the kitchen where food was distributed. The line was long, but each of us got half a loaf of white bread, and we ate it all; we were so hungry that we could literally have eaten a whole horse. We had been more than three weeks without substantial food. Anyone who has never been very hungry cannot know how we felt. My hunger was so intense I still remember the feeling.

We asked ourselves, "What is the situation here? When and how will several thousand people be taken to the ships, and what chance do we have to get on?" We had only negative answers.

The next morning we decided to explore the water narrows and activities around that area. We could see only one ship for wounded soldiers, and four barges crossing the narrow water loaded with military vehicles. We developed some interest in these barges, and returned when it was dark. We hid behind a fence in somebody's backyard.

From that location we could see the barge operation pretty well. There was a continuous flow of military trucks and some smaller vehicles. Germany military police were guarding the operation, and with a flashlight they checked the cargo in the vehicles getting on the barge. One barge could accommodate four large trucks. At two o'clock after midnight they changed the guards.

The next day we said, "Let's go over tonight and study the activities some more to see if they are repeating the pattern."

Everything looked the same and around one-forty-five after midnight the guard started looking tired and walking the opposite direction from the barge. We made a move and jumped inside one of the trucks with a canvas over the top. We acted on instinct. How lucky could we be! We found inside the truck all kinds of ropes. We pulled ropes over our bodies; our hearts were pounding. It was not the first time we had been scared, but we were now really deserters from the German Air Force. We had to wait an hour crouched under the ropes until the truck drove onto the barge. The truck started, then stopped as the light from a flashlight started moving over the ropes and canvas. We held our breaths, praying that we were covered well enough so they wouldn't see any part of us. A few minutes later, the truck was on the barge, and we started floating across the narrows. By the time we got on the other side, daylight was breaking. Somehow we had to get out of the truck before it got too far down the road. We were lucky again that "our" truck was the last one on the barge, so we could jump out with no one behind to see us.

The morning was sunny and brisk. All we could see were white sand and small shrubs along the road side. The road was winding along the sea. When the truck slowed down to make a left turn, we jumped into the white sand and hid behind the shrubs for a short time to see if it was safe to walk. We were walking and hiding when other trucks from the barges were on the road. This narrow land strip would take us to the city of Danzig, where we wanted to go, and we would be west of the Russians. Approaching the city, we were very careful not to expose ourselves to the military police. The streets were full of them. We looked like civilians, but young, and each of us had two legs and two arms. It was unusual to see people looking like us walking on the street, and they could stop us at any time. We were hiding in the daytime, and very slowly moved from one location to another. We were looking for the railroad station, but it wasn't easy to find.

The city had been bombed several times, and damaged buildings were our hiding and sleeping places. We were hungry, and I noticed a sign on the street, "Food for Refugees." We had found hats earlier and used them to hide our faces and to look older. We put them on and walked to the food distribution center. Good looking girls were giving out slices of dark rye bread with cottage cheese on top. It looked so good. After a long wait we got our food. By this time both Johan and I had our clothes hanging on us, we had lost so much weight.

We heard the girls at the distribution window inform a couple of German women with kids that there was a building for refugees where the floors were covered with straw for sleeping. We were refugees and we wanted some decent sleep, at least for one night. We went to that building and we found an empty room and straw on the floor like the girl had said. We lay down and immediately fell asleep. After awhile somebody kicked me in the butt. I raised by head and opened one eye; there were two German policemen with rifles pointing at us. I stood up fast and pulled out my document with the eagle stamps on it and explained that we were refugees from Latvia escaping the Communists. They let us stay in the room with orders to report in the morning to the police building that wasn't far from where we were. Going there would be like committing suicide. As soon as they left and walked in one direction, we were walking fast in the other. We went back to the bombed buildings for our shelter. Somebody had no doubt reported us. We probably looked too healthy.

We found the railroad tracks that led us to the station. We didn't go in, but hid outside until after dark, and we heard the train blow its whistle. Then we jumped on a bumper between cars. After the first train stop, the area was not as congested as before, and we decided to take a chance. At the last minute we walked inside. There it was much warmer and more comfortable, and we didn't run the risk of someone seeing us hanging on outside. We wanted to go as far west as possible, and three times we changed trains at different cities. The last train took us through Berlin and we stayed on that for another two hours going southwest.

We were approaching a town called Th_rsneck. The country looked nice, and we were very hungry. I said, "Why don't we get out and look for a farmer to get a job and some food." Johan agreed. We didn't see any soldiers in the city and it was quiet without shelling and bomb explosions. It was the end of February and it had started warming up.

We walked inside the station and saw a man working there. We asked if he knew a farmer who needed help. He said he could find one for us and asked us to wait. About an hour and a half later, a horse and buggy came with two men in it. One of them said that he was a burgermeister from dorf such and such. Neither Johan nor I knew what these words meant, but soon learned. The burgermeister was the elected official in a small farming community, rather like a mayor in a town. A small farming community was called a dorf. In that area in Germany, a dorf farmland was sub-divided like a pie. All farmhouses were built around the center, forming a large circle. The elementary school, church, tavern, park, playground and social hall (like a small city hall) were built in that circle. There were about two hundred people living in the dorf. The city, Th_rsneck, with a railroad station was about three miles away. They took us to the social hall, and about ten farmers were waiting for us. Some of them were women whose husbands had been called into the service. We stepped out from the buggy and stood there for about ten minutes until they decided who would be getting whom.

I was picked by an older farmer, and Johan was chosen by a woman. My farmer looked like a typical German profile on a postcard. My first impression was that he was not friendly. In his family were his wife and a daughter, about seventeen years old. She was a knockout with deep brown eyes. His three sons had been in the military service, and two of them were killed in the war. He showed me my small room upstairs with a bed and down comforter about twenty inches thick. I was not allowed to see Johan, or to go to other places except work.

It was late afternoon when I knew where I'd be sleeping that night, and I was looking forward to a simple, normal life. I was so hungry, I went downstairs and begged for food. The farmer's wife said that meal time was past, but she would make me a sandwich. The farmer told me that in the morning he would show me what to do.

I lay in bed, closed my eyes and tried to remember the last time I slept in a real bed; it was over two years ago. Here at the farm I was feeling much safer than I had for a long time, and my thoughts went home to my family. Were they still in Latvia, living under the Germans or Russians? I had no way to send or receive a letter, and it would be too dangerous anyway. The war wasn't over yet, and I had no idea how long I would be living here at the farm.

The next morning the farmer woke me up early and showed me the horse and cow stalls with a straw/manure mix on top of the concrete floor. The animals were out in the field. With a long-handled fork I had to pull out the mix and spread it evenly in a compost pile. The big ox (castrated bull) was waiting for me. I had to put a harness over his head and attach a rope. I was standing in the middle of the compost pile, and the ox was walking around and around to pack the compost. I had never seen an ox replacing a horse. The ox was heavier but dumb. Once in a while the farmer sprinkled some kind of powder to reduce odor.

The farmer said that every morning when I finished this job, I could come for breakfast, and later I would be working in the field. The farmer's family ate breakfast earlier, but I was not allowed to sit by their table. I had a table in the corner. Food was on my plate, and that was all I got. The food was good and better than I had for a long time.

The compost pile was in the middle between farm buildings. It was of concrete construction, about five feet deep and about thirty feet round. The ground between the buildings including animal stalls was covered with wash-out rock concrete, with the exception of areas for trees and flower beds. Chickens and pigs had their place behind the buildings. I liked this arrangement; it was easy to clean with a garden hose, letting the water run into the compost pile. Clean-up was my job. Surprisingly, there was very little odor from the compost pile. Compost was used as organic fertilizer for fields, and was made from organically processed straw, left-overs from processing wheat and rye stalks, mixed with animal manure available at any time. The Germans didn't waste anything.

It was spring time and the fields needed to be plowed and prepared for seeding wheat, rye, and clover grass for animals. Plowing the fields was my job and I was given my "favorite" animal, the ox. I learned control words in German, but maybe my ox had difficulty understanding my accent. Many times he didn't listen to me, and especially if shrubs were present. I had to wait until he finished eating all the leaves; then when he got around to it he followed my commands. After a while I got used to him and got the job done.

I was wondering how Johan was doing. I didn't have any way to contact him.

One day I had a surprise from my old farmer employer shouting at me and calling me a traitor and other words I couldn't understand. From the beginning I didn't know what he was talking about until I realized that somebody in his family might have found my "soldier book" that I was hiding in my room. I checked in my room, and it was still there. Of course, that didn't mean they hadn't seen it.

Two days later, I was called to come home from the fields. I found a man in a brown uniform with a swastika band around his left arm sitting in the living room. I knew he was a Nazi Party member. He started asking me all kinds of questions. I thought he wanted to establish my identity in comparison to my "soldier book." The first time the farmer had asked my name, I forgot about my new name on the Latvian ration book, and had given my real name (on my "soldier book.") I was happy now I had done that; otherwise it would have been even more complicated. Then the Nazi asked me to come outside to his red Porsche, and said that he had engine trouble. I opened the hood and seeing the air-cooled engine, I was ready to start taking it apart. I started the engine, and it was obvious there was nothing wrong with it. I knew that he was testing me; if I was really a pilot in the Luftwaffe I should know a fair amount about engines. He said, "That is fine," and he left. I didn't know what would happen next. My conclusion was that the old man had reported me after he found my "soldier book." He couldn't believe that I was in the Luftwaffe with my poor German. He had never heard of Latvia. I don't know why the Nazi didn't arrest me for not being with my unit. Good luck again.

After that, the farmer was not happy with me. I was working six days a week, and Sunday mornings I was taking care of the animals and the compost pile. If I pushed hard, by noon Sunday it was done, and the rest of the day I had time to take care of my own chores, such as laundry, sewing, etc. On Sunday the week after he called me a traitor, his beautiful daughter came, while I was still in the hay barn, carrying a box of dirty family working shoes and said they needed to be cleaned. I said, "Leave them in the box and tomorrow (Monday) I will take care of it." She said that her father wanted them that day. I explained to her that these shoes would take a couple of hours, and Sunday afternoon was my only time off. When I went for lunch, there was no food on my table. I knew where the chickens were laying eggs, and where carrots, cabbage, and other vegetables were available, so I did not go without food.

Monday I went to see the burgermeister and explained my situation. He asked if I wanted to work for another farmer. I was surprised how friendly he was to me. A woman was my new farmer, and she was friendly, too! I didn't have all the rules I had at the old man's place. I could go visit Johan any time I wasn't working, and I could sit by the same table as everyone else.

Johan seemed to be satisfied with what he was doing, and he was the kind of person who could get along with everybody. From the news we knew about the American and British invasion of Normandy. They were fighting battles and winning ground in France and Germany. With Johan I quietly celebrated this news.

One day at the beginning of May 1945, the news was spread; the Americans are coming. We couldn't wait to see a real American! Around this area we didn't see any German military units, and nobody expected any resistance. Tanks began slowly approaching town leaving dust clouds behind. All the dorf population, including my old farmer, were on the streets.

As the tanks passed through the town, American soldiers were sitting on top of them waving and throwing Hershey bars to German kids and good-looking young ladies.

The Germans didn't have big smiles on their faces, but silently they accepted being taken over by Americans instead of Russians. It was a hard war, many lives were lost and homes destroyed. For some time they had known that Hitler's days were numbered. There was some happiness and relief in just knowing that it was all over. At least for two Latvians it was a day of joy and liberation.

We prayed and thanked God for keeping us alive and for giving us freedom.

11

American forces progressed about sixty miles from the farm, occupying part of Berlin, the capital city of Germany, and the city where Hitler had killed himself.

Officially May 15, 1945 was proclaimed the end of the war.

Posters with attention to refugees from German-occupied countries were placed in the city, Thürsneck, and at the surrounding farms. These stated that Patton's U.S. 3rd Army in the city of Leitz would be opening refugee centers to provide assistance and guidance in the days to come.

Stores in the cities would be open to refugees for clothing and other items for personal use. We were thrilled and excited about the news that Uncle Sam was concerned about us.

The clothing we were wearing every day was some left-overs from the Luftwaffe: shoes, socks, and underwear, from the Latvian family we had met on the road: our trousers, shirts and pullovers, and from bombed-out houses on the way: hats. We had been wearing these same clothes for months. It had been very hard to keep clean, but we had done the best we could, washing our clothes and ourselves in whatever water was available. I had been used to being very clean at home.

I picked out a dark blue suit and black shoes and a couple of shirts. Johan found a gray suit, but had a problem finding shoes; his size was very large. I said, "Johan, if you didn't have large feet, you never would have won the bronze medal." He laughed and agreed. We offered to pay; we had some German marks in our pockets from Luftwaffe days when we were getting paid monthly. The storeowner said, "The purchase is on us," and we said "Dankeshön." I don't know who actually paid for those clothes, but it was a good feeling that someone cared about us. We didn't leave the store till everything fit us perfectly. Our old clothing we put in a bag, planning to help the farmers for a few more days.

We felt and looked (we thought) like million dollar men. On the way back to our home, we met my old farmer's daughter with the dark brown eyes and the two Bürgermeister's daughters walking in the other direction. They smiled and said something to each other. We walked over and shook hands for goodbye. We felt good!

Living for almost three months at the farm, I had developed some sentiment for the people. I even understood my old farmer for his anger and for calling me "traitor." His two sons were killed in the war, and in his mind I should have been fighting rather than just working on his farm. He knew nothing of my story.

The day we were ready to leave for good I asked the lady farmer if I could take my pillow with me; she agreed. I packed my bag and we started walking. The refugee center was about ten miles from the farm. We were used to walking.

At the refugee center were several hundred people, and more were coming from every direction; young, old, men, women and children from Poland, Czechoslovakia, Yugoslavia, and the Baltic States. Everybody had a story to tell of how they managed to get there. We met many Latvians, but no one who knew my family.

We were assigned to a two-story military building with a full kitchen and mess hall. The good food was served military buffet style and we could eat as much as we wanted. I ate a lot.

We were told that in the middle of June, DP (Displaced Persons) Camps would be established at various locations, and trains would take us to our designated camps.

Original registration was done the first day of our arrival, identifying us by name and nationality. I had discarded my Karlis Zarins document a long time ago; it had served its purpose. I kept my "soldier book" in my sock. This document I had to hide. If the Americans had found this paper identifying me as a German Luftwaffe member, I would have been put in a prisoner-of-war camp. Americans at that time had no understanding of the Latvian position and situation during the war.

The day came when our train was waiting for us. The announcement was made that train #2 would be for people from the Baltics and Poland, about eight hundred total. Johan's and my name were on the list. There were more trains scheduled at different days and times.

The train blew its whistle and started puffing and picked up speed. For people from the Baltic States -- Latvia, Estonia, and Lithuania -- the assigned DP camp was Augsburg in southern Germany, about 280 miles from the Refugee Center, forty miles from the city of München (Munich) and sixty miles from Austria.

A new organization was formed in cooperation with the 3rd Army called UNRA for helping war refugees. Most of the personnel were volunteers from church groups and other social organizations. All planning and organization, as well as people distribution, was done by that organization.

We were on the train riding for about two hours, and suddenly it stopped in an area surrounded by farm fields. There were no farm houses in sight; it was desolate. We didn't receive any explanation why the train had stopped. Everyone began immediately wondering and worrying about what was going on. We stayed over one night and then another. I said to Johan, "Are you ready to start walking?" He said, "Let's wait a little longer." We and all the people on the train were extremely nervous and frightened. We had been through so much, and real freedom and peace of mind were finally almost ours. We were worried because no other trains passed us or were visible in any direction. What could be wrong? If there was any kind of trouble, I wanted badly to be out of there, on my own, where I believed I had at least a chance to survive. I decided to wait for one more night, but no more.

The next morning, a woman and a man started walking from one end of the train to the other carrying a brown bag, and collecting anything the train riders had to give: gold wedding rings, watches, coins, or any other valuables we had. We were asked to please, please contribute whatever we could. Many of the people, including me, had nothing, but I saw others giving their treasures into the brown bag.

The people doing the collecting gave us what information they had. All trains had been stopped and ordered not to move. A recent agreement had been reached by the major victors in the war, the English, Americans, and Russians as to how Germany and Berlin would be divided. Three zones were established, and we happened to be in the Russian zone.

My heart sank! When I thought of all I had been through trying to escape the Communists, that I might finally end up trapped by them was too horrible to contemplate.

I thought later of the dangers the train engineer risked to take us out of the Russian area against orders. After doing this he could not return to the area he was leaving, either. He may have left family behind. Our only hope was that we could raise enough treasures to somehow make it worth his while to disobey orders and take us.

Apparently it worked, because we were soon under way again. I have often wondered what happened to the other people taking trains to the DP camps. Did they get through safely? I never heard.

From the train station, we were taken by military trucks to Hoffeld, suburb of the city of Augsburg, and we entered into the large two-story building complex. Some of the buildings were damaged by bombs during the war.

A number of buildings were assigned to the Latvians, others to Estonians and Lithuanians. The buildings were designed with a number of small dwelling units in each. Every unit had a separate entrance with a hallway and a small kitchen, and a small bedroom on each side of the hallway with doors. The arrangement accommodated different groups of people: two singles, two married couples without children or one couple with children. The kitchen was shared. However, there were too many people for the available units, so many of us were more crowded than the plan called for. It was no problem. We were so happy to be there.

Close to these buildings was a large fenced-in airport with a number of buildings along one side and several big guns (80's). We were familiar with these guns. This airport, during the war, was used for German Messerschmidt fighter plane development and testing, including the first ME-120 turbo-jet fighter planes.

Buildings inside the fence had been used for development and assembly facilities and a complete line of manufacturing.

Outside the fence, buildings had been used for military personnel and civilians with families who participated in development and research type work there.

Now these buildings were assigned to the war refugees and called DP Camps. In the Latvian facility there were some people occupying rooms already. Kalnins, one of my countrymen, his wife and son were among them. He was chosen by the 3rd Army and UNRA to be the camp organizer and person in charge. He was well qualified to help Latvian refugees, being an attorney who spoke English, German, and, of course, Latvian fluently. For some time he had lived in the USA. Besides more refugees arriving frequently from Leitz, more were expected from other locations. A list was made and rooms were identified by names. From the beginning a family with two kids and Johan and I were assigned to one unit. We decided to take the kitchen, and the family shared the additional rooms. We were not expected to do any cooking in the kitchen, anyway. To eat we had to go to the mess hall. Bathrooms and showers were also located elsewhere.

The day we arrived when I stepped out from the truck I heard someone calling my name. I turned around and my buddy, Guntis, from Technical School was standing there. What a surprise! I said, "What are you doing here?" He replied, "I beat you, and got here first." He was living in the city and asked me, "Why don't you come over tomorrow? We have lots of things to talk about."

He pointed to the streetcar that I could see from the camp. He said, "Go left till you see a big church. At 11 o'clock I will be waiting for you." I said, "See you tomorrow."

We settled into our place and went to the supply building to get blankets; that's all we needed. In the morning I went to the kitchen for breakfast and had noodle soup and bread. I asked the lady in the kitchen if I could have some extra bread, explaining that I would be going to see my friend, and I needed something to eat for lunch. She gave me a third of a loaf of bread and some bologna sausage. I found a knife in the kitchen; it looked to me like a good bread knife, so I packed it in the brown bag with the bread and bologna. I went to the streetcar station and recognized the church that Guntis had described to me. He was waiting for me and said, "We have to wait for another streetcar that will take us to my place."

We were standing talking and waiting for the streetcar to come. Two American M.P.'s (military police) came up to us and asked us to go to the church entrance door, where their motorcycles were parked. I thought they were joking, but they started searching our pockets. One of them looked in my brown bag and told Guntis to leave and told me to go inside the church. They started asking questions: my name and where I lived. I said, "Sir, I just arrived yesterday, and I am in a DP Camp somewhere in this city, and I don't know the address." He had never heard of displaced persons nor the camp. Then he asked me for identification papers. I said, "Sir, I don't have any. I lost them in the war." He told me to take a chair and wait.

I waited for two hours, worrying the whole time, till German city police arrived and took me to their station and put me in jail without asking any questions. I had a question, though, "What am I doing here?" My mind was full of confusion. Either nobody could understand me, or they chose not to answer.

My jail cell was very small and ugly; it didn't even have a floor, just dirt. I stayed overnight, and in the morning, "Berta," the vehicle for transporting prisoners, arrived. Three of us from the police jail were escorted to "Berta" by armed policemen. We were driven somewhere in the city for about an hour before stopping. The doors were opened, and I could see a big three-story building with high entrance steps, like the White House in the USA. Above the entrance were large letters engraved in granite which said, "Criminal Jail, City of Augsburg." I was not a criminal; why was I here? We were "escorted" inside and on a high pedestal was a log book three feet high, and, unfolded, three feet wide. We were logged in and received jail "pajamas." In separate rooms we took off our clothes and put all our belongings into a bag. I was taken to my cell. I felt very strange in "pajamas" in a cell. I had never been in jail before. I felt humiliated and bewildered.

My cell was on the second floor, small with two cots bolted to the floor, and a toilet. On the outside wall was a small window with bars, high up from the floor. I could see only tree branches, moving when the wind was present. The door was solid with a small peek-in window; it opened once in the morning, when the day's food was delivered, and in the afternoon in and out for my allowed half-hour walk at the bottom of a solid ten-foot high fence with barbed wire on top.

Food was the same every day: a round loaf of bread, about six inches in diameter, margarine, and a pitcher of water.

I didn't have any outside or inside communication with anybody. It was a very strange feeling to be cut off from the rest of humanity. When I asked something of the guards they were like mummies, and didn't say a word. Only on Sunday they asked me in German if I would like to go to the church service in the hallway. Some distance away from my cell, the hallway was expanded to a wider area. There were at least a hundred men on one side, and about the same number of women on the other for the service. Just to see some people was a relief, although we weren't allowed to talk to each other.

All day every day I was trying to figure out why I was there, and how it would end. I thought I had finally reached freedom, and here I was in danger again. I was so frustrated. I had nothing to do to make the time go by fast, and over and over I was reading what had been written there by previous prisoners. There were names, dates, time, wisdom of life, and many female forms drawn there.

One day, after thirteen days, the door opened at an unusual time and my "room-mate" was brought in. At least for a while I had someone to talk to. Of course, we didn't have the same language, but we managed. He was from Poland, had been living with his girlfriend, and had a pistol. He broke up with her, and she reported him to the authorities. There were signs posted in the cities for the final date when all weapons should be turned in to the American authorities. He had not obeyed this order. At least he knew the reason he was here.

Soon after this, I was released. No explanation was given for my arrest nor for my release. My cell door was opened, I was pointed in the right direction, given my clothes and a place to dress, and I was out.

I got outside the jail, sat on the steps and started thinking in which direction I should go. I knew I was about an hour from the big church, but I couldn't even remember the streetcar number from the DP Camp to the church.

Augsburg was a large city. I had money for the streetcar, if I could just reason out where to start. I thought that the jail wouldn't be in the city, probably in the suburbs of Augsburg, and the big church was probably in the downtown area.

The first person I saw on the street I asked for the closest streetcar stop. Several people were waiting at the stop. I asked again what number I should take to downtown, and a person asked "Konigsplace?" I said, "Ja, ja," hoping that was the place I wanted to go. Two hours later with two streetcar transfers I was at the right place; I recognized the big church. I didn't see any American M.P.s and I felt fairly safe. So far, so good. Now if I could find the DP Camp about twenty minutes away, I'd be home. It shouldn't be too hard to find, I thought, even if I had to take several different numbered streetcars back and forth; eventually I'd find the DP Camp. I was lucky again, and when I saw the fenced-in airport, I knew I had made it.

When I walked into the room, Johan said, "It looks like you are still alive." He was worrying about me ever since I had been gone. A couple of days after I didn't come home, he went to the see the camp commandant, Kalnins and asked him if he knew about me. The answer was "no."

A few days after my return, when I started attending school, my classmate was Kalnins' son, Karlis. To try to find out why I was put in jail, I asked Karlis if he had heard of a DP being in jail the day after he arrived. He said he had heard, but suggested I see his father. Mr. Kalnins was a tall and very distinguished looking man. He shook hands with me and said he was sorry he couldn't help me sooner. About a week after I was in "pajamas" he received a notification paper from the German city police that one DP from his camp was in jail. The charge was carrying an illegal weapon after the posted date. It hit me then -- I had been carrying a bread knife the day I was arrested. American soldiers couldn't tell the difference between a German military knife and a kitchen knife. As soon as Mr. Kalnins cleared this point I was free. I was very thankful that I didn't have to spend the rest of my life in jail.

During my absence all Latvian facility buildings were occupied and we had a community of over two thousand souls who had escaped Communism, leaving the country on ships and boats and on foot. All their belongings that they could take were in a bag they could carry.

For each building, a person was chosen as the building master overseeing people's needs and trying to accommodate them. A number of people who had never met each other before were now living in the same unit.

The building master was responsible for assigning duties to building occupants so that each person did his or her fair share of regular building maintenance as well as outside care of grass and trees. Besides building and yard work, we had other assigned regular duties, such as working in the kitchen, showers, office, supplies, and whatever else was needed as defined by Kalnins, our camp commandant.

One day I went to the city steam room and shower facility, and I had to wait for room availability. An older lady was sitting next to me; she looked like a DP, maybe from my country. We started talking. She was taking a seedless orange with her to the steam room and would eat it while sweating. She learned from Aryan Yoga while traveling that doing this reduced the pulse rate. She was an interesting and intelligent woman. In Latvia she was a school principal and would be a class master in the newly organized school. She said if I was interested to come and see her. Available seats would be limited. Her name was Mrs. Peterson.

I was asking myself after two and a half years being in a hostile environment, how I was feeling about myself and how I would be able to sit in a classroom and have anything in common with boys and girls who had just started maturing. I was very much aware of how much I had changed since I left my parents' home. My experiences had aged and matured me rapidly. I was not the same rather innocent and idealistic person I had been. Would I be out of place among young people who had not had my experiences? I decided the only way to find out was to try.

So far education hadn't even entered my mind till I talked with Mrs. Peterson. I started developing motherly feelings about her; I missed my own mother. The next day I went to see her, and a seat in the class was already reserved for me; she had been sure I would be coming to the school. She helped me in many ways to stabilize my mental attitude. It is one of the sadnesses of my life that so many people who meant a lot to me were lost as my life went along. She was to some degree one of them, as were Konrads and Johan.

I wanted to review calculus, physics, and other technical subjects. I entered at the third level. The teaching staff had high credentials back home. Several professors from the University of Riga were teaching there.

It was the right decision for me to go back to school and prepare myself for the future. In the class we had both boys and girls. It was the first time in many years that I was in the same class with girls. I liked seeing their smiles; they cheered me up for the rest of the day.

One day several uniformed Russians arrived at the DP camp and settled into one of the buildings. They opened an office. We couldn't understand what business they had to be there.

1946 -- Augsburg, Germany.
In Displaced Persons Camp.

Latvia was taken over by the USSR at the end of the war, and they believed that all citizens belonged to them. After the war we had asked for asylum, and couldn't be returned by force. Only if some individual decided voluntarily to return, he had to see these Russians and go home. They promised a safe return and no retribution, but nobody believed them. As far as I know, nobody returned. This exercise was also needed for formal Displaced Person status and formal protection by the U.S. 3rd Army. Very soon, the Russians packed up and moved back from where they came.

The Americans established a transport plane base in a nearby airport. For the DP's work was available at the base, and many signed up, including Johan. He said, "I am too old to go to school and I like American dollars."

My life started to be a daily routine: school, studies, assigned chores, and some social activities. My thoughts were often going back to my home in Latvia and my family. I started also missing my belongings, including my violin, and wanting answers to questions about my family. What had happened to them during the second Russian takeover? Were they still alive? Did my brother lose his arm? These questions were driving me crazy now that I had time, and all my thoughts did not have to go to survival.

We were warned not to write any letters back home. The Russians wouldn't deliver them, anyway, and knowing that family members left or stayed away from the country and fled to the west was a punishable crime and family members could be sent to labor camps in Siberia.

Everybody in the camp was looking forward to positive change, such as emigration, and we understood that the DP camp was only an intermediate island until permanent settlement somewhere in the world. We didn't know when the doors for emigration would start opening.

In the meantime, life was pretty pleasant and leisurely, and it was up to each individual what he wanted to do. Cultural and sports activities started growing at a fast pace. Theater groups were assembled and the main participants were from the Opera House in Riga, bringing quality performances, and teaching the younger generation this form of art. Everybody had time and the opportunity to master what he chose to do.

The chorus attracted many people to participate, and every year we had a song festival. Singing was a popular activity in Latvia. Groups of singers from other camps arrived to join in our chorus. Artists young and old impressed the public with their paintings on display in an art gallery. Volleyball and basketball games were played constantly.

Romance was in the air as in any other place. I remember a girl, Tana, in my class. She was a champion swimmer. Tom was a tall, good-looking athletic young man, and he was a very good basketball player. After dating for about a year, Tana was playing basketball and Tom was swimming. They got married.

Our spirits were high, as we contemplated a new life of freedom. All were homeless, and brought to the experience as "displaced persons" only their own personal characteristics, but no material possessions. Each person, whether young and with few past accomplishments or a former lawyer or university professor, was starting a new life, and we were all equal in that place, each contributing what he could to our life there. We were the same in that we had been forced to leave all that we had, and each of us carried a certain burden of grief. This created a sameness about all of us, as we understood the sadness we all felt under the cheerfulness of our daily attempt to begin again.

Life was very simple. Once a day we went to the mess hall and filled up our containers with macaroni soup.

Bread and butter we got once a week. We washed our clothes often and we all looked pretty good. Nobody tried to look better than anyone else. Cleanliness was important to all of us; almost every time I wanted to take a shower I had to wait.

Our class physics professor, Dr. Drillis, was also interested in psychology. He didn't waste any time, seeing his opportunity to have a large crowd (camp residents) for the study of human minds and behavior. In the camp, nearly everybody knew everybody. Professor Drillis lived on the second floor. Along the sidewalk, trees were planted some distance apart, and he had measured, so he knew precisely how far apart they were. He sat on a high chair with a note pad in his lap, close to the windows so that he could see the sidewalk. He collected data: the person's name and how long it took for the person to walk between the trees. He learned a lot about those people by his observations on a daily basis. From his studies and observations, he was able to categorize three groups of people, and to predict each group's behavior by how they walked. After two years he published a book. Another trick he liked to play was starting a rumor and waiting to see how long it took to come back to him and how much it had changed. I admired our physics professor, and felt that I was able to understand and remember what he taught. He was one of my mentors.

There were times when I was sitting by the window, watching cheerful appearing people passing by and wondering about them. The population of Latvia was about two million and sixty thousand made it to the DP Camp. Some escaped their homes but didn't make it out of the country or to the camps.

Women with small children, whose husband and father never came back from the war, who gave them the strength to leave their home with a child on one hand, and a bag of possessions in the other? They faced very hard times on the road to the DP Camp.

Older people, where did they find the courage to leave everything behind, to pack a hand bag and walk away from their lifetime homes and possessions?

Professional people, such as attorneys, medical doctors, etc., who gave them the hope to leave many years of education and established lives behind, just to pack a small bag and walk away?

Young people, such as I, who gave us the courage to leave behind our parents and families, with only the dream of making a new life somewhere?

Especially, my thoughts were with the farmers, how hard they worked for themselves and to have good property for their children. Farms had for many years and generations belonged to the family. Where did they get the strength to pack a bag and just walk from their family's land?

I didn't have any answers. I could only speak for myself. It wasn't easy, but when my own life and my family's was threatened, I found the strength for survival.

Many DP Camp residents didn't have personal identification papers, as these were lost in the war. A procedure was established to obtain papers. Two witnesses were needed to identify a person. UNRA officials then signed this document. After I received my official ID papers, I felt I was an official person again, walking on the earth as a recognized citizen. Finally, I could get rid of my "soldier book" identifying me as a German Luftwaffe member. I remembered how alone and humiliated I had felt after my arrest when I had no way to prove who I was.

Soon after class graduation in May 1947, a sign was posted on a bulletin board that Captain Moxley from the U.S. 3rd Army would give a presentation in the mess hall. The subject: the possibility for Latvian and Estonian war veterans to join the 3rd Army for guard and engineering duties.

Many questions entered into our minds. Who wants to wear a uniform again? Are Americans planning more fighting in Europe, or is this just a nice gesture for the Allies?

The other side of the coin was: We'd be paid, have good food and have PX privileges. The advantages won out.

Several hundred signed up from our camp, myself included, and I'm sure many others from other camps. Several Latvian platoons were formed, and my platoon leader was Captain Kalnins. American trucks with white stars arrived and we were ready to go to the city of Giesen, about twenty miles north of Frankfurt.

Back to the barracks, bunk beds, and the high fence surrounding the base. I was in the military environment again. One good thing, I liked the way the barracks were laid out and surrounded with trees. It was pleasant enough.

The first thing I noticed about Americans was that they threw away as much food from their plates as they ate. Peanut cans from the PX were often thrown away only half empty, and if a button was missing from their pants, they thought nothing of throwing the pants away. They were so wasteful! I thought that they must be from a different planet.

It was very satisfying to have American dollars in my pocket. Good money with buying power. In reality, at that time, cigarettes from the PX had more value in the black market than money. The exchange value rate was based on a pack of cigarettes. They could be traded for anything; if a man wanted a woman, the price was one pack, or three packs for an eighteen jewel Swiss hand watch. Cigarettes could, of course, be purchased by us at the PX. It was the third time in my life when money didn't buy anything on the open market: the first time was Latvian lats after the Russian occupation, the second time was Russian rubles after the German occupation, and the third was German marks after the American occupation.

I especially liked southern Germany. Schwarzwald close to the French border, the German Alps meeting the Austrian border, and Bodensee, with Ludwig XII's castle close to Switzerland were all wonderful places. My decision to join the U.S. Army was the right one. I was able to see many places in Germany that wouldn't have been possible otherwise.

I wished that Johan would have joined the army, but he stayed at camp and tried to emigrate to Sweden.

During the month we sometimes had assigned duties on weekends and holidays; if our name was not on the list, we were free to leave base, logging in our names and destinations. This was when we did our extensive sightseeing of Germany.

One weekend my buddies and I decided to see Hitler's "Eagle's Nest" and his headquarters in Berchtesgaden, south of the city of Salzburg. Hitler's other headquarters were in Berlin, but most of the time he and his staff were at this location. "Eagle's Nest" was high in the mountains on top of a very steep road. During Hitler's days, only two vehicles especially designed for that road were able to get to the top. The road was closed, and we couldn't see the "Nest." Sometimes they called it "Hitler's Teahouse."

Six headquarter buildings were bungalow style, about five miles south of the city Berchtesgaden in the foothills of the Alps. Every one of these buildings was connected to underground labyrinths. It was a confusing network of passages including invisible closed wall entrances. Only a few people knew the codes to open the entrance. These labyrinths led to the city of Berchtesgaden with passages spreading in all directions. This complex network was built by Jewish prisoners who were killed when it was finished; the structural plans were also destroyed. Only a few people knew the secret.

A guide with a kerosene lantern led us into the labyrinths and warned us not to separate from the group; we never would be able to find the way out. The guide was leading us to Hitler's underground room about thirty feet below the bungalow. Approaching his room, the labyrinths started widening, and a solid wall "L" shaped, with machine gun windows, was visible in front of us. Behind the walls were Hitler's SS bodyguards when he was alive.

Next to Hitler's room was the room of Eva Braun, his girlfriend. Hers was about the same size, all concrete construction. A slide connected the bungalow to the underground room. The slide allowed a person to get down from the above-ground level in a few seconds. As young men do, we wondered if Hitler ever made love in this room.

Another favorite place we liked to go was Garmisch-Partinkerchen, a typical southern town, where men were wearing leather shorts with suspenders and green hats with pheasant feathers. People living in that area had full necks; the explanation was that drinking mountain water from streams containing too much bromine (mineral) affects glands in their necks. They were happy people, who liked polkas and other dancing.

Town competition started in early spring when snow just started to melt on some hills and the flower, "Edelweiss" started blooming. The first man who could find one and bring it to the town became a hero. The celebration in the town lasted for a week. Some taverns had been especially built like big beer barrels tipped on their sides, with entrances at both ends of the "barrel." The "barrels" could accommodate fifty to seventy beer drinkers. This town's skiing areas were among our favorite places to go, and there was something unusual about them. On top of the hill it was warm, and many people were skiing without shirts. The snow was powdery, good for skiing, and their skins never got sunburned, but turned coppery brown. Many Olympic skiing competitions were held close to this town.

The mountain tops were connected by heavy cables, allowing mountain gondolas to be transported from one top to another. Each gondola could carry about eight people. The last mountain top was Zugspitze, the highest Alp's point on the German side. The Alps mountains were stretching into Austria and Italy.

I don't remember the altitude, but on a sunny day we couldn't see the base of the mountain. The tops were surrounded by the clouds and looked like one continuous snowy mountain top. When we got to the top, a sign pointed to the copper-bronze sphere about five feet round, the same as the cross on top. The cross was the highest point and the sphere was attached to the rocks. Plateaus were about forty feet square and looked small. Very little snow accumulated on top; I believe the wind kept blowing it away. We started looking for a way to get on the plateau raised about five feet from the other surface and covered with lots of snow.

It was scary, but we were determined to touch the cross. Finally, we found the metal cable in the snow that allowed us to pull ourselves on top of the plateau. Once we got on top, it was too frightening to walk. We crawled to the cross and inscribed our names on the sphere. There were so many names, we had to look for a place to write ours. It was interesting to think of all the people who had managed to crawl up to the sphere and cross, and had inscribed their names where ours were also now written.

Oberammergau was a unique city having a religious "Passion play" every ten years. The whole town participated. They each knew the role they would play and lived their lives accordingly to prepare themselves. Sheep, goats, cows and horses were in the foothills everywhere and eating peacefully in the natural surroundings. Motor vehicles were not allowed in the town, but could be parked in a nearby field, and a horse and buggy would take tourists to town. The people wore unique clothing, and didn't cut their hair or shave; the women didn't wear any make-up. Sun colored copper-brown faces and long dresses looked very attractive. The town was in the hills with mountains in the background.

The play was in a natural setting, and the extraordinary performance was unforgettable. Tourism and selling hand-crafted souvenirs were the townspeople's only income. In the town there were no hotels, but people offered to have tourists stay in their homes and have meals with them. After the war, Hollywood producers offered large sums of money to film the Passion Play. It was a cultural tradition for centuries, and could not be bought for any amount of money.

Many songs and stories were written about the River Rhine. The river started flowing from the Swiss Alps and crossed Germany and the Netherlands, entering into the North Sea.

We visited Heidelberg, a city on the Nectar River bank that was known as a student town. The movie, "The Student Prince" with Mario Lanza, the great tenor singer, was filmed here. The River Nectar flowed into the Rhine River, close to the city of Stuttgart. This area was called the wine country.

On the west bank of the rivers Rhine and Nectar, terrace-like grape fields were growing. The west bank of the river was exposed almost all day to the sun. Boat rides on the Rhine River to see wine producing grape fields in progressive flat steps were very impressive and beautiful.

At the military base in Giessen we stayed until August 1948, and then moved to the city of Mannheim base. This city was in the wine country close to Heidelberg. After six months the unit was transferred to Kaiserslautern base, which consisted of U.S. tank training fields and a large depot.

The city was close to the border of France, and in our free time we liked to drive around and see the country. We stopped by the Saare River close to the city of Saarbrücken. The river was small in that area, running along the French and German borders. The weather was nice, and we decided to go swimming.

On the French side of the river we noticed a lady and two daughters fishing from the shore in an area where the water was shallow and water lilies were growing. They threw their fishing lines between lilies, and after a short time they pulled them out with something on the line; they put their catch into a bucket. Our curiosity was growing, and we swam across the river to find out what they were catching and, surprising to us, the bucket contained large green frogs. I asked the lady what they were doing with the frogs. She replied that they would eat the frog legs, and that they were a delicacy. I had never eaten frog legs, and they didn't appeal to me.

And so we spent our time in Germany in the U.S. Army rather pleasantly.

After the war, Germany was sub-divided into the Western Democratic Republic of Germany and Eastern Germany, which became part of the communist block of the Soviet Union, USSR. Western Germany was sub-divided into an American and an English zone. There were no restrictions on travel between the English and American zones.

1949 -- Kaiserslautern, Germany With U.S. 3rd Army

Eastern Germany borders were patrolled by the Russian military, and entering into Eastern Germany required a visa; in most cases it was impossible to obtain one. In Berlin, the Russians built the famous Berlin Wall from concrete blocks, so that westerners couldn't see what was going on behind the wall. At least, that was the reason we heard. The wall effectively made prisoners of the East Berliners.

Southern Germany was part of the American zone and northern Germany was the English zone. Much of my time was spent in the southern part. There were at least twenty DP Camps for the Balts in the American zone, which were protected by the U.S. army, and about a dozen in the English zone, protected by the British army. There were no DP camps in eastern Germany, controlled by the Communist "People's Government."

I had the opportunity to visit almost all Latvian DP camps in southern Germany. Each reminded me of a little

Latvia, having cultural and traditional activities the same as I remembered. It didn't matter which camp I went to see, and I loved visiting them. I especially enjoyed dancing with girls who were speaking my language.

Many times my buddy, Arnis, came with me; after a few drinks he was the funniest man I ever knew. Listening to and watching him cracking jokes and standing at the front of the band eating a fresh lemon without blinking an eye was too much for the band and they had to stop playing; their mouths were puckered up, imagining themselves eating the sour lemon. He was so funny, he added a lot of good humor to this period of my life.

On a number of occasions I was invited to my camp in Augsburg to attend weddings, christenings, class graduations and to see Mrs. Peterson (at school we used to call her "Puke," meaning flower.) I was not the only person who loved her. All news of the happenings in camp during my absence, I received from her. I liked her sense of humor so much. She always had good news and bad news to tell me. The bad news was that at a birthday party about ten people I knew were drinking home-made vodka. They were taken to the hospital not feeling well. Three of them lost their sight. One of them was a girl, Rita, who I knew pretty well from school.

Alcoholic drinks were too expensive to buy from stores, but homemade vodka was available at much less cost. To check out its strength, the liquid was lit, and a light-blue-colored flame indicated just the right strength. The guilty bottle was bought from a Lithuanian man who worked for the Americans at an airport close to the camp. A barrel of methyl alcohol was sitting there and he read "alcohol" on the label; he decided to add some to his brew until it showed a light blue flame when lit. The liquid was transparent and looked the same as the vodka in stores. Methyl alcohol was used as an additive to aircraft cooling systems to prevent freezing. He didn't know the difference between methyl and ethyl alcohol. Ethyl alcohol is a hydrocarbon radical and can be consumed by humans; methyl alcohol cannot.

Later on one man from my unit married Rita, and they settled in a small town close to the city of Giesen. One weekend they invited me to their home. Rita opened the door and let me in. She was more beautiful than ever and was nicely dressed. I was surprised at the neatness of their home, considering she was blind. I couldn't get any words out of my mouth. It was so sad seeing her, and she couldn't see me. When she spoke, in her voice I could hear peacefulness and acceptance of her life. They were dreaming of immigrating to America. For a long time, they were in my mind, reminding me of her tragedy. The war had caused so many tragedies of all kinds, and I was reminded again of how lucky I was to go through so many experiences and to have escaped physically untouched.

It had now been over four years since the last time I had seen my parents, and still they didn't know if I was alive or not. I had the same questions about them and my brother. These past four years, two in the DP Camp and two in the U.S. Army, had gone fast for me. Now I was waiting for the day when I would know where in the world I would be living for the rest of my life. Maybe I would even have my own family and a house where I would be able to raise my children and plant flowers like my dad had done in the front yard back home.

12

In the month of June in 1949 I received a letter from the DP Camp indicating that many countries were opening doors for refugees. The procedures that we had to follow were outlined. We had been waiting for this official news for a long time and were ready to start a new life in a country that wanted us. The countries available for immigration were the USA, Canada, Australia, New Zealand, Belgium and West Germany.

To start processing emigration papers we needed a sponsor. To immigrate to the country chosen, refugees had to satisfy affidavit requirements.

The UNRA agency, consisting mostly of volunteers from churches and other social organizations, were looking for sponsors in their countries who would assume responsibility for the immigrants. The sponsors would provide guidance and assistance for us to find jobs and places to live until we were firmly situated in our new country. The sponsors were individual persons, farmers, contractors, hospitals and employment agencies. The list of potential sponsors and work applications were available at DP camps and were updated daily.

The Latvians in the service who found a sponsor and wanted to start emigration had to receive discharge papers and a service performance statement from the U.S. 3rd Army. After this was done, we were released from the service and returned to the DP Camp to await our emigration date. The sponsors list was sent to us, and we noticed that we were receiving leftovers from the camp with a limited choice of sponsors. I kept hoping that the next one would be better, and that there would be a sponsor available for me.

I started thinking how little I knew about these wonderful countries that were offering me a new home. I had to choose one, but which one?

I remembered the sailors from U.S. ships bringing imported goods to my country and teaching us kids to play baseball.

I remembered from history class about Australia being very great in size and the last major continent to be discovered by Europeans.

I remembered the stories about New Zealand from the Latvian sailors who were sailing all over the world. They told us that New Zealand was a paradise on earth with very attractive tropical scenery and a relaxed lifestyle. In my childhood I always wondered how coconut, banana, and orange trees looked and how the living would be in a tropical climate without the snow and cold temperatures.

I remembered Canada as the second largest country in the world with a surprisingly small population.

I wished that I would be able to see these four countries before I chose one, but that was only a dream. Maybe I should flip a coin and let a piece of metal decide where my new home would be. My final analysis was that it was not so important which one I chose; they were all good countries. Maybe I should let my fingers do the walking on the sponsors list, and then see if I could get one interested in me.

After reading the newly posted sponsors list on a bulletin board, I happily shouted, "New Zealand, New Zealand will be my new home." A farmer in New Zealand was sponsoring six men for farm work. I didn't have any doubt that I could qualify.

In my childhood I had played lots of soccer. I went through the tough Luftwaffe boot camp, and I had survived long walks with Johan trying to escape Russians during the war as well as the farm work I had done. This had kept me in good physical shape. I felt that I could take hard work at the farm if that was necessary to start my new life. Six of us from my unit filled out the affidavit forms answering all the personal questions asked about us. We sent these to the UNRA office at the DP camp in Augsburg. We were told that UNRA personnel would be reviewing the forms for completion and sending them to the potential sponsor for acceptance. We were very careful filling out the forms. If they were not completed properly, they would be sent back and could delay the emigration process. If the sponsor accepted the potential immigrant, the UNRA assigned a number to the affidavit. This number was a substitute for our names and was used all through the emigration process. After receiving the number, we had to apply for discharge from the U.S. Army and return to the DP Camp.

We had high hopes that all six of us would be able to stay together at the sponsor's farm. We wanted to see who would be the first one dating the native girls, who we imagined would be wearing grass skirts and coconut shells.

I was one of the first choosing this sponsor and was happy having a form in my hands and hopes for my new home. If I had second thoughts about this chance for New Zealand and had waited a little longer, I was afraid all sponsors would be taken, and I would be left out. No one knew when the next sponsors list would be available. Most of the men in our unit still didn't have a sponsor.

I started dreaming about my new home in New Zealand and tried to figure out how many oceans and seas would be separating me from my parents' home. I counted the North Pacific, Indian, South Atlantic, and North Atlantic oceans, and the North and Baltic Seas. When I put my finger on the map at the Baltic Sea, the water felt so warm and inviting but it looked so far away from New Zealand, I asked myself how I would ever be able to return home.

We were expecting that in a month's time we would hear from UNRA whether or not we were accepted. The months passed by, second and third, and we were concerned about what had happened to our affidavits.

Finally the letter arrived from UNRA indicating that the sponsor in New Zealand didn't qualify to have immigrants work for him, so we had to look for a new sponsor. We were surprised and disappointed that the person who was willing to help immigrants couldn't qualify to be a sponsor.

In our unit we had an old sailor, "Smart Alex," who said, "Remember, you are not trying to stay in Europe, but wanted to go to one of the Australian Islands. This is the place where some tribes are taking white men's scalps, and cannibals eat white men's flesh. UNRA didn't want to end your lives that way and did some checking." We didn't believe his story. We had heard, though, that in the past some farmers hadn't treated farm help fairly and UNRA had denied their sponsorship of any more immigrants. Perhaps that was it, but we never found out the real reason.

I remembered some time ago reading strange stories about tribes living in Australia who never lay down to sleep, but slept in a sitting position with two feet on the ground and hands crossed over the chest. Australia and New Zealand are neighboring islands in the Pacific and Indian Oceans, separated by the Tasman Sea; they are about one thousand miles apart. I thought perhaps they are too much different from us, and it's just as well we weren't going there. Our dreams about our new home and the native girls with grass skirts went out the window.

Then another surprise came -- it was announced that all DP camps would be closed at the end of 1949. Only the persons with affidavit numbers would be able to stay at a DP camp in 1950 to complete the emigration process. The refugees who didn't choose to leave Europe or didn't satisfy affidavit requirements for health or other reasons would be absorbed by the German economy. They would have to find work and a place to live by themselves. For a single man to find a place to live was easy if he chose to live with a German woman. I didn't.

I started getting desperate to find a sponsor and realized that I needed better communication with the DP Camp; my hopes were higher to find one directly through them. I wrote a letter to Mrs. Peterson. She was still active as a class master and teacher at the school. I explained that I didn't have a sponsor, and I wanted to emigrate. It didn't really matter to what country, but the USA was my first preference.

Soon I received a letter from her. She said that she had two U.S. sponsors for me: Sterling Steel & Wire Company in Sterling, Illinois, and Uldis and Skaidrite Kalnins, New York, New York. Uldis and Skaidrite were my classmates in the DP Camp school. They got married and immigrated to the USA in early 1947 with Uldis' father, who was by profession a jeweler and previously had his own jewelry store in Riga. He had a friend living in New York City, also a jeweler, whom he had known for many years. He became a sponsor for Uldis' family. They were able to proceed with early immigration.

Mrs. Peterson was trying to stay in touch with all her children (students) and wanted to know where in the world they all would be in the future. She was communicating with Uldis and Skaidrite when they lived in New York. Mrs. Peterson never asked for an emigration affidavit, but one day she received one from them, and in the accompanying letter they explained that they wanted to sponsor her to come to the USA and to live with them. Mrs. Peterson was not in a hurry to leave Europe, and she wanted to teach as long as one student remained in the class. Teaching was her life, and she loved it so much. She realized that life would be very empty for her without a class to go to in the new country.

She offered Uldis' and Skaidrite's affidavit to me and said in the letter that she would find another sponsor when she was ready to immigrate to the USA. Being in her fifties, she was concerned about her health, and she said, "Maybe I will never be able to pass the physical tests required for emigration. God will decide for me where I will be living the rest of my life." She didn't have family or relatives who escaped, but she did have many friends who admired her; I was one of them. So many times I thought about her positive attitude toward life. Any time I was troubled about something, her inspirational talks gave me a new energy to overcome my problems.

I didn't have any natural interest in learning a new language and always seemed to have more important things to do. Mrs. Peterson knew this about me. On one of my birthdays she gave me a book with a handwritten note inside the cover saying, "Learning a new language is discovering a new world." When I was facing the new world I wished that I had spent more time learning the language I knew would be spoken where I was going.

I chose the Sterling Steel & Wire Company as my sponsor, and completing the paperwork went smoothly. When I received my affidavit number for processing emigration, I said to myself, "Soon I will be an American." After I received my discharge papers from the army, I returned to the DP Camp and went to the building where Johan and I had been living in the kitchen. I knocked on the entrance door, and the couple with two children were still living there. They told me that Johan had recently immigrated to Sweden. I knew that he had been dreaming about Sweden for some time, and I was glad it worked out for him.

Sweden wasn't one of the countries that offered immigration to refugees after the war. However, during the period when the Russians were taking over the Baltics for the second time, many Latvians tried to escape on boats crossing the Baltic Sea, and they asked the Swedes for asylum. Later, having lived in Sweden for several years, they applied for citizenship and became Swedish citizens. Johan probably knew someone in Sweden who helped him find the right channels to immigrate to that country. We had wanted to go there when I was in the Luftwaffe. I remember the morning we were sitting in our planes and wanted to fly over the Baltic Sea to Sweden, but didn't have enough fuel to cross the sea.

Johan had shared so many experiences with me. I wanted to hear about him again. I knew he was living somewhere in Sweden, but I didn't have his address. After I immigrated to the USA he didn't know where I was, either. There were times I thought about how to find him, at least to be able to send him a Christmas card or maybe even wedding congratulations. I wondered if he was still dreaming about the gold medal in the next Olympics. I'm sad to say that I never did the necessary research to find him. I've never heard of him again. That's one of the really sad side-effects of war: you can be so close to a person, even sharing near death situations, and then everyone scatters to be seen or heard from no more. I'll always be a bit sad that I let Johan slip away from me. He was my companion during my worst days.

The DP Camp was a little thinned out when I arrived, but there were still many people living there. Some had emigrated already, and some had found a girlfriend or work and decided to stay in Germany. I didn't have to sleep in the kitchen anymore; a room for me was available. Some thousands of displaced persons from my camp were in the process of emigration. That included Latvians, Estonians and Lithuanians and people living in the city who wanted to emigrate. Latvians called Lithuanians brothers because they had a similar language.

To process emigration papers was a slow ordeal. Most of the time was spent waiting, waiting for the next step to take, scheduling and rescheduling appointments with different offices. There were many steps the emigrants had to go through before they could see the ship taking them to the Wonderland. I can see now how the technology advancement wonder, the computer, would eliminate or greatly simplify much of the confusion when dealing with such a large crowd in such a complicated process as immigration to another continent.

The potential immigrant to the USA started out with an IRO medical examination, then an American doctor consultation. This was followed by a DP commissioner interview, then a U.S. consultant interview, and finally a CIA interview. Each emigrant was responsible for all documents to be properly completed and signed by the authorized person(s). If there were any problems going through these steps, then the DP had to re-schedule a new appointment and try again. I didn't know one person who went through all the steps without some problems. Most of them were created by the emigrant himself because of language problems or misunderstandings. During the process some people were eliminated for health reasons.

After all the signatures were accumulated, the folder containing the documents was taken to the inspector, who verified that everything was complete and correct. Finally the DP, by his affidavit number, was scheduled for immigration.

U.S. Navy ships were used for the immigration to the United States. After unloading soldiers in Europe, they were filled with immigrants for the return trip.

People waiting to emigrate said, "Immigration to the USA was like a camel sneaking through the eye of a needle."

I made an appointment for my physical, and several weeks later my chest was x-rayed. Another week later I saw the IRO doctor for my complete physical. IRO personnel were DP's with a medical background -- doctors, nurses, x-ray technicians, etc., who were qualified to perform physical exams. I didn't anticipate any problems because I felt fine, and in addition, about six months previously I had had a complete physical, courtesy of the army, as required once a year.

Each time I returned to the camp I felt like I was coming home to little Latvia. It was a bit sad as the streets started getting emptier, and emigration became the focus of almost every conversation. Before, the days had just gone by easily, but now there was eagerness and anticipation in the air. I loved the feeling that I was in the midst of Latvians, but knew that we were close to the end of this period of our lives.

It seemed to me that the people in general were dressed better and more fashionably than two years ago when I was living in the camp. I especially noticed the girls, of course, some of them having grown from kids to good-looking young ladies.

I was walking to the building where Mrs. Peterson lived, and I passed by a partially damaged building from the war and noticed smoke coming out in several places. It couldn't be fire; there was nothing left to burn in that part of the building. The smell in the air reminded me of the smokery where my mom used to send me to get freshly smoked herring for breakfast. I had to satisfy my curiosity and explore what was going on behind the partial wall with no windows, doors, or roof. Loose bricks were all over the place, and I had to climb over a pile of them to get closer to the smoke. The old saying, "There is no smoke without a fire" was true. I saw a man with a long stick turning over pieces of wood in some kind of sophisticated stove. I sat down, and we started talking. His name was Valdis. He explained the principle of a good smokery and the importance of having a long air draft duct for controlled smoke temperature to produce smoked fish with just the right texture and goldish looking skin color. There were enough bricks lying around to build a good one. Some time previously, flounders were available at a local fish market, relatively inexpensive, and he got the idea to smoke them. The flounder is a flat fish that likes the white sand of the Baltic Sea. They look like delta wing airplanes; by wiggling their wings they propel themselves in the water, and like to lie on the sand near the beach. They wiggle their wings also to cover themselves with sand so that nobody can see them laying their eggs. Many times these fish had scared me when I was walking in the sea and suddenly felt that something was wiggling under my feet.

My new friend Valdis said, "The smoking will be done soon, and why don't we go to my place and have a freshly smoked flounder, some vodka, and home-made rye bread?"

It sounded good to me; Mrs. Peterson could wait for another time for my visit. We didn't have a telephone to call her, and she didn't know I was coming anyway, so one day was much the same as another.

I helped to take out the goldish looking, almost perfect smoked fish, and we placed it in a cardboard box to take home. On the way to his place, Valdis told me that sometimes there were a dozen or more places where smoke was coming out of the building at the same time. Many people had discovered the new occupation fast, and fixed themselves some good meals.

Valdis was an intelligent and interesting man and an officer in the 15th Latvian infantry division fighting Russians. He was captured and taken to an American prison camp because he and other Latvians were wearing German uniforms. It took several months until they were released. Valdis said the food in the American prison camp was better than in the German infantry. Nothing, he said, though, could be as bad as the food and inhumane treatment of Russian prisoners in German prison camps.

His wife and two children were back home, he said, and he was hoping that they had survived the second Russian occupation.

By profession, Valdis was an architect. Soon after his graduation from the University of Riga, he had been drafted by the Germans and assigned to the Officers' Academy. After graduation from the academy, he was sent to the front lines and fought several battles. He was lucky to get through the war without being wounded. When we started talking about our home and country we wondered if she would ever recover from the wounds of nine years. There was a noticeable sadness in his voice, particularly concern about the soldiers who were wounded and were now facing emigration. How many of them would be able to emigrate, and how many would find those doors closed? There was no good alternative for them. The people who had suffered the most physical pain now also felt like pieces of wood washed up from the Baltic Sea and left on the beach for somebody to pick up and burn as firewood. We asked each other why our people had to suffer so much for no reason in the world. We had all been happy with what we had at home and weren't asking anybody for anything.

I was glad to have someone to talk with about the war, especially over vodka and smoked flounder. When I was in it, survival was the main thing I had on my mind, and I was busy just trying to stay alive. Now, though, I had time to think about it, and also to do some reading. Valdis was quite a bit older than I, and had much more information about the Russians and Hitler.

Some people thought that Hitler's decision to attack Russia was the result of a long-standing plan, he told me. Some historians had taken this view, as they noted that Hitler had for years spoken of the coming struggle with Bolshevism (Communism.) This kind of thinking was welcomed by many Germans who were ready to hear what he was saying. The idea of racial superiority had been part of the training of military men for a long time. Hitler described the perfect world as beautiful, decent, socially equal, and full of culture, which should be the German goal. On the other side, he said, there was a population of 180 million (Russia) and a mixture of races, whose names were unpronounceable, and who should be shot down without pity or compassion. These he called animals that torture and ill-treat prisoners and did not behave as decent people would. He blamed the Jews for welding these people into one ideology called Bolshevism. He stated that now there was Russia, half of Asia, and part of Europe overwhelming Germany and the whole world. He taught fear and hatred and his country followed him. Hitler's Germany was responsible for the systematic murder of about six million Jews and hundreds of thousands of people from occupied countries, including the Baltic States, of which Latvia was one. During the German occupation of my country from 1941 to 1944, I knew of people taken by the Gestapo. After the war when I read about the atrocities and about the Nuremberg Tribunal's verdicts convicting the Nazi murderers, I could hardly believe that such brutality could exist between humans in the twentieth century.

Despite Stalin's and Hitler's antagonistic ideologies, the two leaders signed a ten-year pact of non-aggression in

1939. Secretly they agreed to divide Poland and the Baltics between them. Despite this agreement, the Germans attacked Russia in 1941.

I still could not understand it. They seemed insane, and so many people suffered so much because of the insanity. Valdis and I were among the sufferers, as were millions of others. The world should never allow any men to have so much power again, we agreed.

After a while it was time for me to go back to my room; it took me several days to put these sad thoughts out of my mind. When something was bothering me, I had to be by myself to sort it out and to get back my peace of mind. I had to convince myself that there was nothing I could do or change. Since I knew this was true, eventually I was able to face the realities of my life again.

Mrs. Peterson had to wait for another couple of days for a visit from me. She knew from my letter that I would be returning to the camp, and that I had chosen Sterling Steel & Wire Company as my sponsor. The next Saturday I knocked at her door. "Is it you Andrejs?" she called from another room. "Come in and take a chair. I'll be with you as soon as I get ready and do a couple of chores. Please read the paper and give me a few minutes."

I apologized for coming so early. Soon she came out looking like the teacher from my school days who everyone called "flower." She knew what the students called her, and she said she liked that name. She had a bowl in her hand, and said that she had a special treat for me. I asked what it was, and she told me it was blueberries and milk. She knew it was one of my favorite foods; she was always so nice to me. After I ate my treat, and she finished her chores, she sat down and said, "Now we can talk all day." I was afraid of that, as I knew how long talks wore me out. I expressed to her my appreciation for all she had done for me, helping me through my hard times and now for her willingness to give up her own sponsor for me. I had decided not to use her sponsor, but it meant a lot to me anyway. She had also found the sponsor I did use, Sterling Steel & Wire Co. She answered me that she was happy to help me, and for me not to even mention it. Then we started talking about Uldis and Skaidrite living in New York City; they seemed very satisfied with their new life. That they thought so much of her and invited her to live with them touched her heart. When she had received the letter, she was so happy she cried, and told everyone in the camp the news. It was not only the affidavit to emigrate that made her so happy, but just that they had cared enough about her to invite her to live with them. They wanted to give back a little of what she had given to them as a teacher and friend.

I said, "If you choose to emigrate soon, you can use the Uldis affidavit. I am satisfied with my choice, and I want to start from scratch without any help. I have a job waiting for me, and that is the most important thing I need to start my new life." She felt about the same and said, "If I can pass the physical and emigrate, I'll look for a job in a library and rent a small room; that is all I need. I don't want to be a burden to anybody, including Uldis and Skaidrite. As far as emigration, I'll be the last one on the ship. I'm going to stay here as long as I'm needed." No wonder everyone loved her.

I could understand how hard it was for her to think of leaving Europe and planning life in the new country at her age. She said, "We are talking and feeling like April's children; we are strong like Taurus." I didn't understand what she meant. She explained that according to the astrological signs Taurus means bull, and that since both our birthdays are April 24, we were both born under the sign of the bull. I replied that I could never forget her birthday since it was the same as mine.

Mrs. Peterson said that the senior graduation was planned for May, and she would like for me to set up and decorate the stage for the graduation. I told her that I would be happy to do it. When I had been at the school before I had come up with a symbol that was used for all official school occasions, and she remembered that. We talked for several hours, and that was enough for me; it was time to go back to my place.

About four weeks previously I had had my chest x-rays taken, and I still didn't have the results back. I couldn't proceed with my emigration until this step was completed. I decided to go to the motor pool located outside the camp and try to get a temporary job to keep me busy and give me a little money till my emigration was done. The motor pool was surrounded by an open field used for vehicle storage. The facility building accommodated offices for clerical work, communications and dispatch functions. On the side of the building an addition had been built for servicing the vehicles. A man from Estonia named "Lepiks" was in charge of the operation. There were about thirty vehicles. Most of them were army one-half and three-quarter ton trucks and jeeps and about ten station wagons. These vehicles were used to provide services to the Augsburg suburb Hochfeld and Haustetten DP Camps. These two camps were about five miles apart. I was living in Hochfeld. The lighter vehicles, jeeps and station wagons, were assigned to the UNRA and IRS (Internal Refugee Service) personnel for communicating with the other camps to give social help and assistance as needed. These were especially for children who had lost their parents by death. Some of these activities included German and other families in that area. I went to see "Lepik," the motor pool manager and said, "I want a job." He asked, "Do you know how to drive military trucks?" I replied, "I've been in the U.S. Army for over two years, where I drove whatever was needed, so I can qualify to drive whatever you have."

He assigned me to take the international driver's license test. It was required to operate motor pool vehicles. It was about the most comprehensive test I had ever taken. The road driving test was not too bad, but the toys I had to play with to pass the test were complicated. They had a special machine to test the brake reaction speed in different situations, eye aberration for proper focusing at a distance, eye angle perspective and some others. These bench tests took about an hour to complete. I passed all the tests; the next Monday I reported to Lepik as a new driver on his crew.

Every day I was checking for my x-ray results and got the same answer: maybe tomorrow. X-rays were sent to the city for development. Finally I received the answer that I had been waiting for; I had bad lungs with dark spots on them. I couldn't believe it! I also couldn't proceed with emigration until the spots were cleared, which could be several years, I was told. I went back to the doctor and asked him if the lungs could get so bad in six months. If necessary, I could go back to my unit in the Army, and get the results of the test they had done on my lungs. The doctor said that to develop these spots would take a long time, and he would look into the matter. He told me to keep checking with the nurse as to the status of my x-rays. For the time being, my emigration was on hold.

At night I couldn't sleep for worrying about all my hopes and dreams for my new home in America. I had been building these dreams in my mind for some time. I had thought my emigration was assured; suddenly the wind was blowing everything out the window. I was reminded of my dashed hopes for immigration to New Zealand. If other countries didn't want me for health reasons, and if I had to live in Germany, maybe I could find some satisfaction helping to rebuild the bombed out cities where Johan and I had hidden and slept for survival. However, no matter how much I rationalized, the idea of staying in Germany was repellant. I even thought maybe I'd be better off to find a rich German woman. That would solve most of my immediate problems. That was only an early morning dream, however.

The next day I went to see the nurse to hear if the doctor had given information or instructions for me. Even if the nurse had been Marilyn Monroe, I wouldn't have looked at her twice; my energy level was very low. The nurse was from Czechoslovakia. The doctor hadn't talked to her about me. She surprised me when she said, "You don't have to worry; you are young and a non-smoker. By looking at your face, I'm sure you don't have lung problems. People with lung trouble look very pale and unhealthy. There is a possibility that your x-rays were switched with someone else's."

I asked, "How can that be possible, since my name and affidavit number were on the x-ray film?"

She replied, "Money makes anything possible, even buying emigration papers, and exchanging medical records. You wouldn't be the first person that happened to. I hope that's what happened in your case, and I'm sure we'll find out soon."

I could hardly believe what she said. I hoped and prayed that she was right, and it would be cleared up soon.

The next day I was told to have my x-rays re-taken. I then waited for another four weeks to receive the results. Nothing was wrong with my lungs; I proceeded with the next emigration step. I'm sure the nurse was right in her assessment; somebody else emigrated with my lungs. I was so happy I invited her out for dinner. She accepted and we had a nice evening. I almost wanted to blow my top, and make a federal case about my x-rays, but then I said to myself, "So what; I'm on my way to America."

At the motor pool I worked eight hours a day five days a week. If I needed some time off during the week I could compensate by working late or on Saturday. I liked that arrangement. I drove the big truck to the supply depot or railroad station to pick up the boxes of food and other supplies. Then I brought them back to Hochfeld and Haustetten DP Camp supply distribution buildings.

One afternoon I passed the mess hall and heard the chorus practicing Christmas songs, and I realized that it was only four weeks away. My last Christmas at home was in 1942 when my dad and I went to the forest to choose the tree and then decorated it with real white candles. It was now seven years without my family. The year 1949 could be my last Christmas on this continent. The Atlantic Ocean separated Europe from America by about six thousand miles. I felt like a broken branch from a tree whose roots have been pulled out of the ground. I didn't have a home to return to, and soon I would be losing all my friends and the Latvian community. I felt that I needed to be with my people to share our past and future. I tried to think only positive thoughts and to be strong, as I remembered what Mrs. Peterson had said, "We are Taurus, and we have the strength to overcome adversity."

On Christmas Eve I went to the community center, which was our mess hall with a stage built at one end. The nicely decorated tree was next to the stage. The scene on the stage was of snow covered trees and falling snow flakes. Several hundred people were there, and I recognized almost all the grown-ups, but wasn't so sure about the younger people; they had changed so much in the last two years while I was away. Mrs. Peterson was there, and she introduced me to several young ladies from the senior class. One of them in particular was very attractive to me; her name was Inta. Several times when I passed her walking on the street I noticed her sweet smile and the sparkle in her eyes. One day I stopped and started talking to her. She was beautiful and she spoke in a very soft voice. I liked her. She said that her emigration papers were almost complete, but her parents intended to slow down the process until May. After her graduation, they would immigrate to Detroit in the United States. I couldn't resist asking her for a date. She was very definite that I must come to the place she lived and meet her parents, the old fashioned way of dating.

After the holidays more intensive emigration started, and the motor pool trucks were assigned to take the boxes of emigrants' belongings to the railroad station. Some people who had been working had accumulated some clothing and other personal items they wanted to take with them to their new country.

My own emigration papers were moving slowly, and I couldn't predict when I would see the end of the paperwork.

The only spark in my life at that time was Inta. I told her that I would be setting up the stage for graduation, and she said, "I'll help you." We made the school symbol about six feet tall with a black background and silver letters. On the stage it was placed on the left side of the long table which was covered with a white tablecloth; the school director and the teaching staff sat at this table during the graduation ceremony. The symbol was raised about two feet above the floor and was surrounded with flowers that were also on the table and on the side of the steps. Here the students walked across the stage to receive their diplomas. The graduation was nice, and it was heartwarming to have a ceremony with the flavor of home.

Inta was wearing a dark blue dress and looked very mature and pretty. Afterwards, when I was talking to her I remarked that her father looked very familiar, and I asked where he had been during the war. Inta said that he was in the Latvian (German) Luftwaffe. That explained my puzzle; he was a pilot in the second squadron. It was a coincidence that I had met his daughter.

My relationship with Inta was mostly platonic, but a little romantic, too. A couple of weeks after graduation, she told me that her family had received their immigration papers and that three days later they had to be in Camp Grohn. This was the emigrant transition camp, and they had to stay there for a few days or longer until U.S. Navy ships were available to be occupied. The ships were docked at the Bremerhaven port not far from Camp Grohn. I helped her family close the few boxes they had, and with a heavy felt pen I wrote their destination address in Detroit, Michigan. We didn't talk much; there was some sadness between us. She asked if I would like to come to the train with her family. I told her, "Sure, I'd like to." I liked those country trains with large windows, wood varnished benches and holding bars close to the ceiling. I wanted to be with Inta as long as possible and to see the train that would take her to Camp Grohn. The train blew its whistle, and I had to say goodbye, with a kiss and hug for her and a handshake with her brother and parents. Tears were in our eyes and I had to leave the train. I stood outside on the platform close to the window to see her. White smoke started puffing from the steam engine. We waved to each other, and her window started getting further and further from me. I waited till the train disappeared into the dark forest and only the path of the white smoke was visible over the tree tops. I was looking in the sky to see if the white smoke was telling me whether I ever would see her again. The wind cleared the white smoke and all I could see was the blue sky without any message. About a week later I received a postcard from Inta saying that the next day they would be on the ship; in big letters she had written "See you in America." It seemed to me that all I had been doing for years was saying "Goodbye" to people and places I cared about, and with no promise of ever seeing them again.

It was the beginning of June; the trees had new leaves, the grass was green, and the flowers had started blooming. The air was fresh and warm. This time of year was the nicest in southern Germany. I wished that I was in the Garmish-Partenkirchen mountains to see the melting snow and the water streams running down the hills. Maybe somebody had found the first edelweiss flower, and the whole town was celebrating. I couldn't leave the camp, because my name could come up for the next step - interview. The experts were saying that June, July and August were the best months to be on the Atlantic Ocean before the storms started coming. Every day I loaded the truck full of the new emigrant boxes and took them to the railroad station. I was wearing my hand out, shaking hands and saying goodbye to my friends who were leaving. Walking on the streets after dark, there were fewer and fewer lights in the windows. I was wondering if there would still be somebody left in the camp to shake hands with me when I was leaving. I knew that Mrs. Peterson would be there. She was the central person for information about everything. She received many letters from the people who had immigrated earlier, not only from her "children," but also from other camp residents; almost everyone knew her. Sometimes I went to visit her to hear the news, good and bad. She said that most of the people who immigrated to the USA were thankful to their sponsors, and were on the road to being able to stand on their own feet. However, there was frightening news about some families who immigrated to Mississippi and were working for cotton farmers. On their arrival they were provided with some kind of shed; they couldn't call it a house, because through the walls they could see cotton fields outside. When it was raining they didn't know where to put the buckets to catch the rain; it came in every place. Most of these families had small children. They were given beat-up, hardly usable furniture, beds, mattresses, tables, chairs, etc. The farmers set the rent for the house and furniture; the things the immigrants needed, such as food, were purchased for them by the farmer. All this was charged against their salary for work in the cotton fields and they could never catch up. They were like slaves, obligated to work for the farmer for the rest of their lives. It was a very bad situation and they didn't have any way to alleviate it. Mrs. Peterson said she couldn't sleep thinking and worrying about these families.

After I was in the USA I heard more about these people. Their story was spread by many of the Latvian immigrants, who all cared about each other and were deeply interested in all our futures. It seems to me that most immigrants felt the same way. Perhaps that is why so many in the 1920's and earlier settled in communities of their own nationality. For instance, the Lithuanian community in Chicago, Illinois, still occupies an area of thirty or more blocks square. They have their own church and Sunday schools for the children, as well as many other social and cultural activities.

Milwaukee, Wisconsin was another typical city where the bridge divided the Germans on the north side and the Polish on the south.

The recently immigrated Latvians wrote letters and were anxious to help their countrymen in Mississippi, but they couldn't do much; they had no resources -- money, cars or connections to help.

The director of the Memorial Hospital in Milwaukee was an early Latvian immigrant, who came to the United States in the middle of 1930. He had received his medical doctor's training in Riga and for a while he was working in the hospital there. He met a young, attractive nurse and told her that he was planning to immigrate to the USA and promised to come back and take her with him. He did what he promised; they were married, immigrated, and had a daughter. They lived in a beautiful large home, surrounded with trees. They heard about the families in Mississippi and some others who were having a difficult time to get established in the new country. They wanted to help and they did, sending money and train tickets, finding jobs and accommodating the immigrants in their own home while helping them to get settled. Particularly the wife and daughter spent a lot of time helping the new immigrants. In most cases, the money was repaid, and was used again to help others. Their reaching out hands will be remembered forever by those they helped and by many other Latvians.

Finally, I received an appointment for an interview with the U.S. consultant and CIA office. The men were very friendly and said that from my background information I should have a good future in the USA. They asked me what my future plans were. I said, "To have a good education and a challenging job." One of them was an MIT (Massachusetts Institute of Technology) graduate and suggested that I strive to get into that school for the best possible future. We shook hands, and I was ready to board one of the ships I could see in my mind's eye that would take me to the Wonderland.

I didn't have any boxes to take to the railroad station, just a hand bag that I could carry with me. By August fourth I should be in Camp Grohn, the last stop before boarding the ship.

I had to face another sad day with tears in my eyes as I said goodbye to Mrs. Peterson and my other friends who were still in the camp. Mrs. Peterson had passed the physical but was not in a hurry to have exit interview appointments.

The time came for me and several other people from the camp to take a streetcar and go to the railroad station. I knew all along that the DP Camp was only a transitional place in my life, but when I sat in the streetcar and looked through the window as the camp buildings began to disappear from my sight, I realized the attachment I had developed to that place. I had many happy memories of my years there, and part of me hated to leave. I knew that my memories of "Little Latvia" would remain with me all my life, and they have.

The DP Camp was located close to the German southern border and the train had to take us north to Camp Grohn close to the North Sea. The train ride was about four hundred miles and went through the large cities of Nuremburg, Frankfurt, Hanover, and Bremerhaven. Living in Germany for five years, I had had the opportunity to spend time in these cities. At Camp Grohn several buildings were available for the emigrants to stay for a few days to complete the final paperwork. I received my papers saying:

SHIP: USS GENERAL HERSHEY
FROM: BREMERHAVEN TO NEW YORK (USA)
DATE OF SAILING: AUGUST 6, 1950
PASSENGER NUMBER: 62

The next morning we were taken to the port city of Bremerhaven. Several navy buses loaded with emigrants started going through the narrow streets of the old city approaching the port. There was a feeling of great excitement in the air, and people started clapping when they saw the open water, fishing boats, ships, and flying birds. My heart started pounding, knowing this was really it; I was going to America. The bus stopped, and there was a big smile on everybody's face saying, "We made it this far."

When I stepped out of the bus, I took a deep breath, and the air with freshness and smell reminded me of the air near the Baltic Sea, when I played in the white sand on the beach at home. The Baltic Sea, through the waterways surrounding Denmark, Sweden and Norway, flows into the North Sea. Bremerhaven on the North Sea was a port I liked so much; I could have stayed all day watching the big and small boats and ships entering and leaving the port. It reminded me of busy ants going in all directions with their own purpose.

Among all the ships, one was outstanding. It was gray color and slim-looking with a red, white and blue flag proudly displayed on the mast.

With the slight wind that was present, the flag was waving to us. The name of this ship was "General Hershey." We had to wait for a while until all the people arrived; there were mothers with children, men and women with silver in their hair, boys and good-looking girls.

Before we started walking to the ship we received orientation about the rules for the voyage, such as where the men and women would sleep separately, how the food service would be operated, and various other information. The ship entrance walk-on platform was attached; we gave our names and numbers to the Navy boys and they guided us to our quarters. It took me a few seconds to become acquainted with my bunk bed and to stow my few belongings; then I was out on the deck, standing by the rail and watching the European birds flying around. I watched the walk-on platform move away and the heavy tie down ropes slowly being pulled onto the ship. I heard the deep tone of the steam whistle blow, sending the message that the ship was ready to depart. Very slowly the ship started pulling away from the dock, and the narrow water gap, with a few orange peels floating in it, separated me from the European land.

Suddenly, and for the first time since I had started thinking about emigrating, the enormity of what I was doing swept over me. I had a strange feeling of emptiness, as I realized that I was leaving Europe, and would never be able to take a train and go home. I felt immense sadness overcome me, and I couldn't stop the tears. I turned my head in both directions to see if anybody saw me cry. I need not have worried, there were tears in all the eyes around me as they said a silent goodbye to their European homes.

Soon the captain came on the loudspeaker and congratulated all the immigrants to America and wished us all the best in our new lives. I stood by the railing till the city silhouettes disappeared from my sight. The mighty ship was floating in the North Sea waters leaving behind a white water trail. The horizon surrounded me and I was still looking at a dark line with clouds above it. That's all I could see of the land I had just left behind. A voice came on the pager and asked for a dozen volunteers to perform what he called M.P. (military police) duties on the ship. I volunteered and received an M.P. arm band. He explained what to do in case of emergencies and showed us the ship facilities and how to find a doctor and nurse if medical help was needed. A walk through the living quarters, day and night, was needed to see that everything was in proper order. The actual duty for each volunteer was two to three hours per day.

Soon, after the dust settled, we realized that with the crowd of Lithuanians, Estonians, Latvians and Poles on the ship, we'd be living in very close quarters for at least ten days or more. We introduced ourselves to our neighbors. There were only a few familiar faces. Most of the people came from different DP Camps. It was late afternoon when the ship pulled out of Port Bremerhaven, and it was time for our first dinner in the mess hall.

The ship captain said, "In the morning we will be entering into the narrow channel called the Straits of Dover". This narrow channel separated England from France. Dover was a city right at the shore on England's coast. This channel would lead the ship from the North Sea to the English Channel, the open water that connected with the Atlantic Ocean. About six thousand miles sailing would take us to New York.

The first day of sailing was pleasant. The sea was calm and the weather warm. After dinner I walked on the deck and watched the sunset. After an exciting day it was time to find my bunk and catch some sleep.

1950 -- North Atlantic Ocean.
On U.S. Navy ship "General Hershey" on the way to America

In the morning the ship blew its horn on entering into the channel. I went upstairs onto the deck as fast as I could. I thought I would be the first one by the rails, but I was surprised that there were many people before me. The lady standing next to me said that she couldn't sleep during the night and wanted some fresh air. It was early morning daylight, and heavy fog surrounded the English coast; we could barely see the coastline. Soon after the ship sailed through the English Channel, we were in the Atlantic Ocean's open waters. Ocean waves were noticeable, but for the mighty ship they didn't cause any trouble. The people were talking, walking or reading. The kids were bundled up in blankets and were sitting on the deck waiting for the dolphins, whales or flying fish to show up. Everybody was waiting to go to the mess hall for a good meal. It looked like it would be pleasant cruising to the USA.

The fifth day the captain announced that the storm was heading our way, and that in the morning we would be in it. He said, "It's nothing to worry about, but we might be in for a rough ride for awhile."

In the morning we started feeling the rolling waves, and the ship started hitting the white tops of them harder and harder. The rolling of the ship affected many people aboard. There were no motion pills available to protect us from getting seasick. Plastic bags were displayed all over. There was nothing anyone could do about the situation; we would just have to live through it to see the Wonderland. I remember my dad saying, "On the rough sea, concentrate your eyes at one point on the horizon to prevent getting sick." I was practicing what he said, and I kept busy, running up and down the stairs helping the people who needed help. I tried to stay on deck as much as possible so I could breathe the fresh air.

At night I took my blanket and went to the deck, leaning my back against the cabin wall. I was watching the moon trying to sneak through the heavy clouds. There were a few other people on the deck who had the same idea; the lady sitting next to me made counting the stars more interesting. There were times when we got unexpected cold showers, reminding us that we were in rough sea. I was lucky that I was one who didn't get sick. During meal times our mess hall was almost empty because of so many sick people, and I enjoyed eating as much bacon and eggs as I wanted. The storm affected us for four days and slowed down our arrival in New York by a day.

It was our tenth day at sea, and the Atlantic Ocean waves started looking more normal. We began walking without holding onto the rails or whatever we could grab. The eleventh day the captain announced that we were not too far from the New York harbor. Everybody's face started returning to the normal color; most people's faces were very pale during the sick spell. We now forgot all about the recent stormy days.

The Navy crew members wanted to be sure that we didn't have a boring day, so announced that we had to go through the debugging process as immigration rules required before we could put one foot on American soil. Instructions followed: Men to the right, women to the left. Stay in line and wait until we got to the door. After entering the room, take off all our clothes and close our eyes. The Navy boys with the sprayer would then spray us. It was pointed out that after the treatment, we must be sure that we have a paper signed. The debugging took a good part of that day.

I loved my sleeping place outside on the deck. The sea was calm, and the last night on the ship I wanted to sleep in that place. I hoped that during the night as we approached New York, I might be able to see the city lights.

The ship wasn't moving under power, and was floating; the powerful diesel engines were idling. I looked for the city lights but couldn't find any; then I looked for the stars and couldn't see any of those either. Then I realized that heavy fog was covering everything. I looked at my wristwatch and realized that I was looking at Bremerhaven time; I had left there eleven days ago. It was too complicated to figure out what New York time would be. I went to see one of the crew members, and he told me it was four o'clock in the morning. I was wide-awake and went down to my sleeping quarters and picked up the bag with my belongings. I took a shower, shaved, and put clean clothes on; I was ready to walk on New York City streets. It was still dark outside and I had to wait. There was a long hour until daybreak, and then there still was no land in sight. I put my hands on the rail and looked out over the dark water. I thought about the six thousand mile voyage to cross the Atlantic. I especially thought about the brave European men who first crossed this big ocean. Documentary evidence supports claims that the Vikings reached the New World first, about 1,000 A.D. Their ships were built from wood, with flexible hull, keel and sail. Portuguese and English fishing vessels made the crossing during the fifteenth century; Columbus made the voyage later in that century with his ships: the Pinta, the Niña, and the Santa Maria. The storm we had experienced was relatively mild, but our mighty ship, all steel welded construction with powerful engines, sometimes felt like a matchbox floating on the powerful waves. How could those historical ships have survived this same ocean, I wondered.

Soon a voice came over the loudspeaker saying, "Attention, attention, this is the captain speaking." He said that during the night we had idled in the Atlantic Ocean and soon would be docking in New York City at the Manhattan port at the mouth of the river. After departure from the ship, we should look for the letters along the terminal, and go to the one that is the first letter of our last name. The UNRA representatives would be waiting and would provide guidance on what to do next.

On the way to the harbor we would be passing through the lower Hudson Bay with the narrows on one side, and Brooklyn on the right. Then we would be entering into the upper bay. On the left side would be the Statue of Liberty on a small island and further down, Ellis Island. Our port terminal would be about a mile from Ellis Island. It sounded very exciting, and I was hoping that the fog would clear, so I could see all of it.

The ship started moving and almost everybody was outside on the deck by the rails to witness our entry into the

New World. We started seeing land and silhouettes of buildings and skyscrapers. There were many large commercial ships docked close to the Hudson River mouth, and many were entering or leaving the harbor -- Thank God that we had radar to avoid crashing into each other. We passed through the Verrazono Bridge. Verrazono was the first who discovered the river, but Hudson was exploring also; the river was named the Hudson River. The sun helped the fog to disappear, and there was the Statue of Liberty, some distance away heightened by the eastern sun. We locked our eyes to the one hundred fifty one foot tall statue, but had to wait till the ship was closer to see all her beauty. She was in the form of a draped female figure with stretched arm carrying a torch aloft. She was a beautiful sight, and the symbol of all that we hoped for in our new lives. She overlooks the New York harbor and greets the new immigrants. I felt that she was silently saying to me, "You made it; this country is yours." The lady is an unforgettable sight.

Then we were approaching a small island, which was a picnic ground for early Dutch settlers. The federal government purchased the island, and it was named for Samuel Ellis, who owned it. The Immigration Bureau was created; there immigrants were examined and either admitted or sent back to their countries. Twelve million immigrants had come through Ellis Island from 1895 to 1924 when the law was changed, and immigration slowed down.

Now clearly I could see the tallest building in the world at that time, the Empire State Building, the skyscrapers on both sides of the river, and parks along the river bank. It looked to me that the city's physical setting was a very complex assortment of islands and parts of islands. From seeing postcards in Europe I had imagined New York, but I didn't realize that the river would be so wide, the buildings so tall, and that so many ships could find the terminal to dock.

Our ship, the General Hershey, made a right turn and was in the designated terminal. Everything was as the captain had said. UNRA ladies were waiting and waving to us while the sailors tied down the ship. Large letters were attached to the dock posts, and we were ready to depart. I picked up my bag and walked down the steps. When I was down on solid ground my legs didn't quite take me where I needed to go. For a while I felt the ship's up and down motion. I introduced myself to the UNRA ladies by the post "E." One of them said that soon the luggage would be unloaded from the ship and could be picked up. I said, "I have only my bag." She asked for my name and gave me a large envelope. Inside the envelope I found a train ticket with a schedule to Sterling, Illinois, five dollars for food, and a placard with important information: my name, emigration number, home country, destination, and sponsor's name and telephone number. The lady told me, "Don't lose the placard. In case you get lost on the way to Sterling, show it to the police or some young lady, and you'll get help." She pointed out that on the train it would be very important to have the placard displayed. The train conductor would let me know when to get out. I opened my ticket envelope to familiarize myself with my train schedule. The train would be leaving the Grand Central terminal in Manhattan at 9 p.m., and the next night by 10 p.m. I would be in Sterling. The lady told me to go to the designated area and look for the bus with the Grand Central sign displayed. The bus driver would instruct me how to find the train terminal to Chicago.

Sterling and Rock Falls were twin cities on the Rock River about one hundred twenty miles west of Chicago. The population for both cities was less than forty thousand.

I had enough time to find my new shipboard friends in the crowd and say goodbye. I walked to the designated bus area and there were about a dozen waiting. The buses displayed numbers or names, Pennsylvania Station or Grand Central. They were waiting for the immigrants to fill them up. Some immigrants stayed on the east coast, some went west, north or south, wherever their sponsors were located. The Grand Central buses started filling up and I walked inside. When I saw the Grand Central Station building I thought it was really impressive from the outside and inside both, displaying an architectural art style with open spaced columns. The building reminded me of some opera houses in Europe. It was easy to find my terminal, and I planned to be back there about an hour before the train left. In the meantime I wanted to walk on the New York streets and see how it felt to be in this very large city in the USA. I put my bag in a safe at the terminal, but took my placard with me. I didn't display it; I wanted to look like everybody else on the street. I didn't want anybody to know that I had just come from the ship. I was hungry and looked for a place to eat. I had two hot dogs, fries, and a coke. The hot dogs and fries were twenty-five cents each, and the coke five cents. That was my first meal in the U.S. forty-five years ago.

I stood by the street corner watching the cars, trucks, and everything that was rolling by very noisily on wheels. I had never seen so many cars on the street, and I never experienced so much noise either. The smell of exhaust gas from the vehicles was noticeable. I remembered my home town when I would see horses and wagons on the streets and only a few cars. The biggest problem with horses was that they sometimes stopped and left a big blob on the street.

It seemed to me that there must be a fire someplace in the city, and everybody was rushing to get there. They were all in such a hurry.

I liked the clothing stores with stylish suits and shirts. Most of the people on the street were nicely dressed with the women wearing cheerful colored outfits. I did not like the idea of living in the big city, and I was glad that my sponsor's city was small and on a river.

It started getting dark and I returned to the terminal. The train was waiting for me. I put the placard around my neck and walked onto the train. I chose a window seat to see the New York City lights at night and the countryside during the day. I sat on a comfortable seat and thanked God for taking me to America.

So many things had happened in my life after I left home and my family. I wished that I could write a letter to my parents letting them know that I was alive and that I had seen the Statue of Liberty and had just stepped on the land that is the best in the world. I was ready to begin building a new life in America.

13

After I had finally gotten settled in the United States and started my job, I had time to think about the future. I realized I had some basic goals. First, I hoped that somehow, and soon, news of my family in Latvia would come to me. I wanted so much to speak with them, but knew that was probably not possible. In any case, I wanted desperately to hear of them, and for them to know I had lived through the war, and that the love and support they had given me in my early life had made me strong enough to survive. My other goals were: a family, including a wife and children, a home where I could put down roots and have a yard with flowers like my dad had, and I wanted challenging and rewarding work.

When I was living in Milwaukee in the fifties, I received regularly a U.S. published Latvian newspaper, as did all the immigrants, who were eager for news of home. The newspaper cautioned us time and again not to try to contact relatives in Latvia, as things there under the Communists were not good. In 1949, deportations to Siberia or other Russian hells were twice as many as in 1941. The people's land was taken away and communal farming had been established. Some farmers were not able to accept the situation, they showed resistance, and that was the end of their lives in Latvia. In the late forties all forests were searched by Russian military with dogs, and people were found living there. Most of these had no chance to escape, and that was the end of their lives in Latvia. Some relatives living in Sweden or England didn't heed the warnings and sent papers or letters to family back home.

Addressees in Latvia found themselves in trouble with the Communists and were soon on a train bound for Siberia or another equally horrible life. The people who managed to escape Communism to another country were considered traitors and their relatives left behind were made to suffer. The Communists were again showing their power and real face to the small, helpless, peace-loving country.

The brave fishermen fishing in the Baltic Sea were sometimes able to leak out information to the Swedish fishermen, and later their news was published in the Latvian newspaper in the USA. All the immigrants who read these stories knew that they were true, as we had all lived under Communism ourselves. We were very frustrated and angry that we were not allowed even to know if our families were alive. Most of the immigrants had lost friends and/or family who had been left behind. For myself, I thought of my family every day, and prayed that things would somehow get better there.

After awhile, the newspaper had a column, "Looking for" with the names of people who had left their homes and could not be found, or any people who were displaced by the war.

One day in 1958 when I came home from work, I received a call from a friend saying that my name was in the paper. I impatiently opened my copy, and there was my name! Of course, I speculated as to who was looking for me. I prayed that it was my family back home. The directions were to contact the Red Cross in Switzerland. My hands were shaking as I wrote, but my letter went out the same day.

A month later I received a letter from the Red Cross International in Geneva. The letter was in German stating that my dad was looking for me, but nothing was said about my mother or brother. I was so relieved, though, just to know that my dad was alive and wanted to know about me.

Apparently, some arrangement had been made whereby the Communists were allowing the Red Cross to look for people who were lost to their families, and to put them in contact with people in the USSR.

Now that I have raised children, I understand even more how my parents must have felt having to send a not-yet-eighteen-year-old off to war and never knowing his fate.

It had now been fourteen years since my last meeting with my parents. Of course, this latest development made me think of them even more. Many times I re-lived the last hours I had spent with them. The Latvian newspaper cautioned that all mail to the USSR was censored, so we still had to be careful about what we wrote. I was so happy, though, to be able to communicate with them at all; I cried when I saw my dad's handwriting on the letter he wrote back. Feelings long kept bottled up washed over me, as I realized that finally the hope of my life was coming true; I could find out about my family and let them know I was okay, too.

Dad sent me a picture of himself holding a birdcage he had built. I felt that it was symbolic of their situation -- that they were living like birds trapped in a cage. At least, my family was together, and my brother had not had his arm amputated, but had a plastic elbow joint installed instead. They were all alive and well. What relief I felt!

Through the years since then, my brother sent me the news in 1967 that my mother had died, and in 1973 that my dad was gone also. My brother and I have kept in touch through the years. Life there has not been easy, and was not for my parents, either. My brother told me that my dad had to sell my violin in order to buy food. My aunt, the wife of my dad's brother, was very helpful to my parents in their old age, I was told. I can only hope that their lives were not too hard. There was nothing I could do at that time, as I sent them packages that they did not receive.

Mail to them had to be sent to Moscow, and delivery was dependent upon the government there. Actually, we still have difficulty getting money or packages to our Latvian family. Apparently, mail thievery there is a problem. This is not too surprising, as many people are still having a great struggle to live. Since the dissolution of the USSR, Latvia is once again a free and independent country, but establishing a free market economy is not easy.

In 1990 in the summer, I planned to visit Latvia and my brother and his family. In January I filled out papers with photographs, and submitted them to the Russian consulate in San Francisco for entry into the USSR. Papers bounced back and forth, asking for more information and more pictures, etc. When summer came and I still didn't seem to be close to obtaining the necessary visa, I gave up for then. Somebody at that time, it seemed, did not want me to go to Latvia; I had a top-secret clearance from the U.S. government for my work in the space program, and I wonder if that had something to do with my not getting the visa. The next year I retired and had open heart surgery, and have not felt able to make the trip. I think of them often. My brother's wife, Ilze, is very proficient in the use of English, and she and my friend here have a steady correspondence.

Speaking of re-discovering the past, I must mention Mrs. Peterson, who was such a good friend and influence during my DP Camp days. After fifteen years of my life here, I was notified of a DP Camp school reunion to the held in Chicago. Nothing could have kept me away.

I was living in Huntsville, Alabama at that time, and Ilmars Dalins, an acquaintance from the Technical School in Latvia, and later a friend at the DP Camp and in the U.S. Army, made the trip with me.

Mrs. Peterson had more silver in her hair, but the same spark in her eyes and her voice. Seeing several hundred of her "children," she said she felt like she had gone to heaven. She was living in the Bronx, New York, in an apartment with an older Latvian gentleman in order to share expenses. She had worked for the City Library for twelve years, but didn't have much money to live on in retirement. Some of us visited her several times, and she always had blueberries and milk for a treat, just as she had years ago. It was sad each time we left her, knowing how much she had given of herself to all the young people she had helped. In her golden age she deserved more, but wouldn't accept offers from her students to live with them. She still wanted her independence.

Konrads' life in Sweden was a mystery. I heard about him from people I knew who had relatives there. They recognized his name from Swedish newspapers as a pilot from Latvia who worked for the Swedish Intelligence. Some time later an article in the paper said that Konrads and two others were flying over Indonesia when their plane lost power and crashed; all three were killed. I felt that this story was not true, but I never had evidence of that. I guess I just couldn't accept something so ordinary happening to Konrads.

My second goal was a home and family. I was twenty-five when I came to the US, and when I was twenty-six I met a beautiful young lady named Veldze at a Latvian folk dance in Milwaukee, and we fell in love and got married. She gave birth to my two sons and two daughters, and was a good mother. My children, Dainis, Sarma, Mara, and Imants were born in Milwaukee.

I wanted a home where I could raise my children and plant flowers. About eight months after my oldest son, Dainis, was born, we found an older corner house with a large, grassy backyard, a white picket fence and a linden tree in the back. The house was in a good neighborhood with high rated schools, and was four blocks from Jefferson

Park, the south side of Milwaukee. Each time a new child joined our family, I planted a dwarf fruit tree in the backyard. After living in Milwaukee for ten years, we had four healthy trees growing and a picket fence covered with red roses. We also had four thriving children as of August, 1962.

I remember the days when we went to the city parks or spent time at Lake Michigan. I recall Mara toddling around; Dainis at age six was "troop leader." Sarma was a year younger than Dainis, and Imants can't remember anything about Milwaukee, as he was just three months old when we moved. On occasions now when we all get together, I know that my dream of a family was worthwhile. Being together with my children, their spouses, and my seven grandchildren are the happiest moments in my life. It was worth all I went through to have the life I have now. I have been very lucky once more.

I wanted interesting and challenging work. In Milwaukee I worked for Astronautics Corp. of America. I didn't yet have a formal degree, but with my technical background and three years engineering college credits, I was given the opportunity to be part of the design and development team for aircraft navigational instruments for the air force, navy and marines.

Working closely with the program manager and chief engineer, I successfully designed my first aircraft instruments, BDHI, (Bearing Distance Heading Indicator.) Our next successful designs were: Fuel Flow Indicator and H.S.I.(Horizontal Situation Indicator). This was the most complicated cockpit indicator that the air force had.

A successful design was determined by the ability to meet air force acceptance test criteria without major redesign. I was surprised that these relatively complex mechanical designs with electrical interfaces were easy for me, and my confidence grew. I enjoyed the company's appreciation parties after the completion of a successful prototype qualification test. Having an air force qualified instrument made it possible for the company to do competitive bidding and to win the production contract.

After I got married and had family responsibilities, I had to slow down my education. I was almost always working days and going to night classes at Marquette University, plus studying at home, of course. I finally received my engineering degree, BSME, from the University of Alabama in 1968.

I was chosen for special assignment to work with the chief engineer who had many years experience designing inertial guidance systems. The task was to design and develop for the X-15, rocket plane, an experimental inertial guidance system with star-tracker. Four infrared turret type Smiths cameras were attached to the star tracker telescope. This system was developed for well-known astronomer and professor, Dr. Code, at the University of Wisconsin. The rocket plane, X-15, was attached to the belly of the B-52 bomber and dropped from 45,000 feet, then propelled with its own power. When the X-15 reached a certain altitude the hinged door behind the pilot was opened. The star tracker was exposed to space, and our system took over the plane guidance. The star-tracker was locked to the specific star in space. The programmed infra-red cameras started clicking and taking pictures in deep space. In the late fifties we didn't have satellites, and our three X-15 rocket planes flew to the very edge of our atmosphere (determined by the pressure). I had DOD (Department of Defense) secret clearance.

Space exploration was becoming the scientific topic in the late fifties. On October 14, 1957, Russia launched "Sputnik" into orbit. The unmistakable "beep-beep-beep" sound of Sputnik's radio transmission could be heard, and the reflection from the shiny satellite could be seen over the USA. This event signalled a clear message to the American people that Sputnik could easily have been a nuclear warhead. The nuclear physicist, Edward Teller, referred to the Sputnik launching as a greater defeat for the U.S. than Pearl Harbor. For those who understood the significance of what had happened, the ability of the Russians to send a satellite orbiting into space and around Earth was a very frightening development. The Department of Defense understood well that the U.S. needed to expand its space program, and fast.

By September 1945 the first group of Germans, including Wernher von Braun, were spirited away to New Mexico. By the start of the 1950s, von Braun's group moved to Huntsville, Alabama, where the Army Ballistic Missile Agency was formed. Department of Defense gave the go-ahead to von Braun's team to assemble, within ninety days, a booster (rocket). Scientists at the Jet Propulsion Laboratory in California assembled the satellite Explorer-1. In January, 1958 it successfully reached orbit. In 1958 the civilian agency NASA was formed and von Braun became the director of Marshall Space Flight Center in Huntsville. The Space Race was under way to launch a human being into orbit.

In January, 1961, a test launch of our Mercury capsule ended in disaster when the Atlas booster exploded. Radio Moscow astonished the world with the news, "The first cosmic ship with a man on board was orbited around the earth from the Soviet Union."

Our president, John F. Kennedy, said, "Now is the time to take greater strides in space, time for this nation to take a clearly leading role in space achievement, which holds the key to our future on earth. Our goal is, before this decade is out, to land a man on the moon and return him safely to earth."

We were running neck and neck with the Russians preparing for a moon landing. On December 8, 1968, a Russian capsule with cosmonaut Pavel Belyayev on board was waiting for the countdown for the moon landing. The window opened for the launch, but nothing was launched. To this day, the Russians have not announced the reason why, and Belyayev took his secret to the grave as he died two years later after an appendix operation went fatally wrong. Later the Soviets launched the unmanned Luna 15 three days before our Apollo II moon landing, to collect and return lunar soil. The Russian Luna 15 crashed into the Sea of Storms.

In the meanwhile I was happy with my work at Astronautics and was surprised in 1962 to receive an offer for another position from an old friend mentioned earlier. Dr. Ilmars Dalins had been my schoolmate at the Technical School in Latvia, and then at the DP Camp school. He came to the U.S. in about the same condition as I, without relatives or money. He was very bright and dedicated, and got some scholarships, and also worked at a variety of jobs, including ticket selling for an outdoor theater, McDonald's, etc., as he went through college and obtained a doctorate degree in physics. He then studied at MIT specializing in plasma (nuclear) physics. He later received an offer from the U.S. government to join NASA as Plasma Physics Branch Chief. He wanted to do classical physics research at the University Research Institute. A new laboratory, "Surface Physics" was established and occupied one wing in the Research Institute. Dr. Dalins offered me a position there. He asked me to join the research team to design apparatus for sophisticated experiments and to be in charge of the laboratory operation.

The work at Astronautics was very interesting, and I had a promising future with the company. Also, I didn't know how my family would feel about leaving Milwaukee. On the other hand, to receive such an offer might be a once-in-a-lifetime opportunity. My family decided to take a vacation and find out how we liked Huntsville, Alabama. We liked it. We put our house up for sale, sold it and moved to Huntsville. There we bought a new brick house with large trees surrounding our property; it was like living in a park.

I started in my new position. Research in the surface physics field was dealing on atomic scale to uncover and understand nature better. The main purpose for our studies was to determine ionization characteristics needed to improve engine performance. In the early sixties, the ion (or electric propulsion) engine was very promising for future space travel, but ionization efficiency was low and needed improvement.

After a couple of years of effort, the laboratory was pretty well established. We had our own model shop, full size glassblowing facility, hydrogen furnace, a number of different vacuum systems, mass spectrometer, low electron energy diffraction system and everything else for serious studies. This branch of physics was very difficult, and in the U.S. we had less than a dozen active surface physicists; three of them were our consultants.

On our permanent staff we had four to six research engineers and technicians. We also had three to five Ph.D. research scientists from NASA and three to five National Science Foundation fellows from England and Germany. The latter were doing their research projects in our laboratory. In addition, we had graduate and postgraduate candidates completing their thesis work for the degree. Scientists were thesis advisers. Assistance from university professors was available at any time.

Needless to say, the work there was extremely challenging, and my scientific education was progressing daily, to say nothing of the high level company I was keeping. For a small town boy from Latvia, this was all pretty exciting.

To accommodate experiments we were dealing with liquid nitrogen and helium temperatures (approaching absolute "0.") In the laboratory we had to simulate deep space pressure (vacuum) 10-14 Torr to minimize experiment contamination. To see atomic crystalline structures we needed one million magnification, and only the electron field emission microscope or ion field emission microscope would achieve that. We couldn't buy the microscopes, because our experiments were built inside the glass envelope and each experimental configuration was different. We developed and built the microscopes that were tools for further scientific studies. Many experiments were performed that resulted in publications.

Several times Wernher von Braun came to see our laboratory and shook hands with us. This was very exciting to me, as I consider him one of the greatest minds of our time. He was one of the first rocket scientists, and was largely responsible for our ability to get beyond our atmosphere into space.

Working with scientists was a great benefit to me. I learned so much from them. They even convinced me that dead, dried-out wood is alive, that electrons are spinning in the wood, and that their spin energy determines the physical properties of the matter.

Besides the physics research programs, we developed surface seismographs for studying acoustic waves coupling to the seismic waves from the large rocket firings at Cape Kennedy in Florida. The large rocket was Wernher von Braun's mighty Saturn-5, developed in Huntsville. The rocket with the Apollo capsule as its manned payload was able to put a man on the moon and return safely back to Earth. During the Apollo program, a series of Saturn/Apollo launches was executed from Cape Kennedy.

During the rocket lift-off, large thrust was generated and transmitted to the earth. The seismographs were placed at different locations and seismic activities were measured during these launches.

NASA in Huntsville was being sued by local farmers claiming that when all five engines fired during Saturn static testing, their water wells dried out. In Decatur, twenty miles away from Huntsville, Wolverine Copper Tube Manufacturing Company claimed that windows were cracked on one side of their buildings from testing. NASA wanted us to investigate, using seismographs to determine if there was enough ground disturbance to sustain these claims. They were not sustained.

The seismology program was a good opportunity for us to have some outdoor activities, and we could breathe the fresh ocean air at Cape Kennedy. The seismograph sites chosen were at isolated areas having minimum human and vehicle traffic. Along the ocean were white sand and small shrubs. These natural areas had wild life, and we had to watch out for wild pigs (boars) and poisonous coral snakes. There were times when seismographs were located at Jacksonville, Florida, Skidaway Island, Georgia, and Monmouth, New Jersey.

After landing the man on the moon, the Apollo program was completed and funding for NASA was drastically reduced. The reduction affected funding for the research programs. Many NASA scientists and engineers started looking for new jobs. I was fortunate that the university received a contract from Dr. Gunther, NASA, for mechanical design of the proton spectrometer for the Skylab Spacecraft. We also got another contract from Dr. Tom Parnell, who was Cosmic Ray Branch Chief at NASA. This contract was for mechanical design of the proportional counter and ionization chamber system, for the HEAO-A spacecraft. Dr. Parnell wanted me to be a member of his research team. The work was carried out at Research Institute and NASA facilities. This development was an extremely challenging program which required a considerable effort in the mechanical engineering area, and was a several-year contract to start. After prototype development, balloon flight testing was scheduled in Palestine, Texas. A special gondola was designed to accommodate the experiment. The balloon launch facilities were government operated, and an appointment was needed for the assigned scheduled date. "Tiny Tim" was the name for the balloon launch vehicle. It had two steering wheels, one at each end. An experimental package was attached to the vehicles and the parachute release mechanism was attached to the balloon. The huge balloon was stretched on the ground and slowly filled with helium gas. The balloon started rising and lifted the package of "Tiny Tim." The drivers maneuvered the vehicle to vertically line up the package with the balloon. The balloon altitude was planned for sixty thousand feet. The chaser plane followed the balloon path. It was interesting to see our package taken to the sky to measure and collect data from cosmic ray activities in the atmosphere. Data received from the experiment was very good and was published in monthly NASA reports.

About two months after my participation in the foregoing experiment, three men from TRW, Redondo Beach, California, wanted to talk to me and asked if I would be interested in joining TRW. They left a stack of papers and said they hoped I would be interested. This was another big surprise for me. I was happy where I was and was not looking for a job.

I talked the offer over with Dr. Parnell; he said that as long as NASA was in Huntsville, I had a secure future. He said that TRW was a good company and one of the top aerospace companies in the country. He explained that the proportional counters/ionization chamber experiment was one selected by NASA for HEAO satellite "grand tour of plants," to give insight into the violent processes that occur in the universe which are visible only at x-ray and gamma-ray wavelengths. He said that our experiment performed well, and NASA would soon be going out with RFP (request for proposal) to the industry. TRW was one of the companies expected to respond. Parnell was one of the principal investigators for HEAO payload.

Dr. Parnell was a navy pilot and was still flying in the reserves. That was one of the reasons I liked him, and we worked so well together; it was hard for me to think about breaking up the team. He said if I didn't like the big company I could always come back to Huntsville.

For several days I didn't say anything to my family about the offer. I had to think it over myself. Huntsville had been our home for ten years and a good place to raise our children. It was a special southern city. The Smoky Mountains stretched from Tennessee/North Carolina through the city, and the Tennessee River was a couple of miles away. The 1962 population was 60,000; by 1972 it was 162,000. Everything built was new and modern. NASA's space programs attracted the best scientists and engineers in the country, and good schools were built for their children. I worked in an academic environment I liked. From my office window I could see a pond with swans swimming; many pine trees surrounded the water. Across the road in the Research Park, I could see IBM, Teledyne, and Lockheed buildings. The buildings were not cramped together, but had lots of space between them. Alabama had enough land for breathing. I could travel from one end of town to the other in twenty minutes. The Monte Sano Mountains were beautiful, and every Easter we went to the early church service in the outdoor mountain setting. The white dogwood trees were flowering contrasting with yellow and violet blooming trees, giving the impression that nature was celebrating.

What would be the reason for me to leave Huntsville? More money, better retirement, health and dental insurance. California meant Hollywood, movie stars, the ocean and palms. The life style and weather looked attractive in the magazines. Finally, I told my family we had the choice to move to California. My oldest son, Dainis, was in the Marines, so I couldn't get his opinion. I was surprised that the family wanted to move. There was magic associated with the word "California." My daughter, Sarma, said, "Dad, we don't want to live all our lives in Alabama." So the decision was made, and we put our house up or sale.

We stayed for another three months till I finished a few tasks at Research Institute. Dr. Parnell lived in a beautiful home in Monte Sano, and he gave me a "going-away" party. The house was full of people I knew, and it was a wonderful party.

We arrived in California the first week of July, 1972 and I reported to TRW July 15th. We looked for a house, and found one in Torrance, not too far from the ocean and TRW.

In my new position I worked as a WUM (work unit manager) responsible for mechanical design. When I joined TRW, my department was completing the Viking program development, but I had responsibilities.

For the Viking mission to the Red Planet (Mars), TRW developed a biology processor for investigating enzymes in Mars' soil for the possibility of life on that planet, and also developed a meteorological station for determining weather there.

The ultraviolet spectrometer was developed for the spacecraft Voyager mission to measure the atmosphere and other space activities of Jupiter, Saturn, Uranus, and Neptune. In August, 1989, after twelve years in space, Voyager passed Neptune 3,200 million miles from Earth, still communicating with Earth, but heading out of the Solar System towards the stars.

The knowledge I acquired in plasma and surface physics at the Research Institute in Alabama proved to be invaluable in programs such as Plasma Separation Process (PSP), Special Isotope Separation Process (SIS), Free Electron Mazer (FEM) and others. I had a Department of Energy Q (top secret) clearance and Department of Defense top secret clearance.

In 1985, I was promoted to a management position as a section head with ten engineers in my section.

In October 1990, after eighteen years of stimulating and rewarding work, I retired. These were good years for me, but they went too fast. I could hardly believe that my children were eighteen years older than when we had moved to Torrance. Dainis, after serving four years in the Marines, had joined his brother and sisters in southern California.

When I was thinking of going to Latvia in 1990, I contacted several travel agencies to learn about the airlines that were landing at the same airport where we landed and took off in October 1944. I called a travel agency on the east coast advertising Baltic flights. A soft and sympathetic lady's voice explained in English about the flight arrangements and said she would mail me a brochure. She asked for my name and responded saying, "I can speak Latvian." She said her name was Inta. I wanted to ask her if she was the Inta I had known at the DP Camp, but I didn't. I don't know why. I guess sometimes the passage of time makes it difficult to dredge up the past. I knew of my long-ago Inta that she lived in Detroit, was married, and was active in the Latvian community. I waited for several weeks for the brochure, and felt that I had a good reason to call the agency and talk again with Inta. I was mentally prepared to ask questions this time. I called and asked for

Inta. The lady on the phone said, "Inta isn't with us anymore." She could tell I wanted more information, and said, "She got married for the second time and moved away." The name she mentioned as Inta's last name in her first marriage sounded familiar to me. It seems too great a coincidence, but I felt I had briefly found Inta from the DP Camp.

And so my career is over, and I am living a retired life. I live near the desert where the summers are very hot and the air is dry. All my children live nearby. Summers I am enjoying traveling and spending time in western Washington. The Puget Sound, Straits of Juan de Fuca, and deep water inlets in the area have created many islands and shore lines. Deep water ports in Olympia, Seattle, Tacoma and Bremerton accommodate ocean liners and navy ships. Pleasure boats of all sizes and people fishing are common sights. Taking a ferry from Port Angeles to Vancouver Island and from Anacortes passing through the San Juan Islands are unforgettable experiences. I like to take the ferry from Bremerton to Seattle, and walk along the Seattle waterfront to go shopping and investigating at the Pike Place Market. I was born and raised near the water, and western Washington reminds me of my childhood where I played by the Baltic Sea. Tall pine trees grew there also along the shore line. Bremerton has a naval shipyard and is the city where by friend, Joan, was born and lived most of her life.

One day Joan's son, Bob, invited us for a day on his boat exploring the waterways in the area. Slowly we passed the shipyard docks, where some navy ships are sitting in the water, retired and decommissioned. Loudly we were reading familiar ship's names as we were passing by. I read the name, "General Hershey." The boat stopped, and my eyes wandered over the great ship, seeing rails, decks, and steps to my bunk. I remember vividly all my days on that ship, the most important trip of my life.

Nobody was now on the mighty ship; only seagulls found a place to nest. Rust spots were noticeable, and the hull water line was covered with algae. All was quiet there, but it brought to mind the days when this ship was alive, perhaps with a navy band playing, with sailors proudly stepping on the freshly painted deck, and flags flying on the masts. I thought of my relationship to the ship; we had both survived rough waters, and now were resting and retired after busy lives.

Almost fifty years ago I touched the rails, slept on the deck dreaming of a new life, and ran the steps to the living quarters. This ship had brought me to the Statue of Liberty and all the other wonders of my new life in the United States of America.

Liepaja – My Hometown

The Baltic States

Made in the USA
San Bernardino, CA
26 October 2015